Editor
Eric Migliaccio

Cover Artist
Brenda DiAntonis

Illustrators
Clint McKnight
Mark Mason

Editor in Chief
Ina Massler Levin, M.A.

Creative Director
Karen J. Goldfluss, M.S. Ed.

Art Coordinator
Renée Christine Yates

Imaging
James Edward Grace
Rosa C. See
Craig Gunnell

Publisher
Mary D. Smith, M.S. Ed.

S0-BFB-189

Differentiated Lessons and Assessments
SCIENCE

Grade **4**

Includes Standards & Benchmarks

Focuses on:

- Reading Strategies
- Content Specific Vocabulary
- Multiple Assessment Options
- Activities for Various Learning Styles
- Graphic Organizers

Author

Julia McMeans, M.Ed.

Teacher Created Resources, Inc.
6421 Industry Way
Westminster, CA 92683
www.teachercreated.com

ISBN: 978-1-4206-2924-8

©2010 Teacher Created Resources, Inc.
Reprinted, 2014

Made in U.S.A.

Teacher Created Resources

Table of Contents

Table of Contents *(cont.)*

Table of Contents (cont.)

Introduction

 ## What is differentiated instruction?

Just when you thought it was safe to go back into the classroom, yet another new teaching strategy emerges, one which will demand more of your time, more of your energy, and endless hours of professional development. Just kidding!

The truth is that the only thing new about differentiated instruction is the name "differentiated instruction," for teachers know that every time they give a student a few extra minutes to take a test or allow a child to draw a response (as opposed to writing one), they have differentiated their instruction. Simply put, differentiated instruction means that the instruction of the core content, the student activities, and the assessments are modified to meet the individual needs, styles, and abilities of students.

 ## How is instruction differentiated?

Instruction may be differentiated or modified using multiple criteria, including (but not limited to) learning style, reading level, interest, ability, and language. In addition, an educator may differentiate all components of the lesson—content delivery, student activities, and assessment—or only some of them.

 ## How can this book help?

This book contains a lot of strategies, activities, assessments, and resources, but how you use them will be your decision. Some of them you will be familiar with, others you will not be. Some will work for your students and others won't. No one knows your students as well as you do, so ultimately you will decide what you can and cannot use.

This book is intended to help you differentiate your lessons. It is not the last word on the subject of differentiated instruction, nor does it contain every possible strategy known to teacher-kind; it is just one more tool to add to your box.

How This Book Is Organized

This book is divided into nine units. Each unit contains the following sections:

 ## Teacher Materials

The teacher materials provide the following:

- **Key Unit Concepts:** These are the important ideas, events, and people contained within the student briefs that should be emphasized during the teaching of the unit.

- **Discussion Topics:** These are one or two topics related specifically to the unit that you may use to generate discussion before you begin the unit proper.

- **Assessments:** Here you will find a list of the assessments that are provided for the unit. There are many ways in which to differentiate the assessments. Explanations of these strategies will be cross-referenced with page numbers.

In addition to the above features, the following generic strategies are given on pages 8 and 9. These strategies can be used with each unit and will be referenced in the Teacher Materials section of each unit:

- **Vocabulary Activities/Strategies:** Use this list of suggested activities and strategies to further your students' understanding of the vocabulary words presented in each unit.

- **Building Background:** Here you will find some generic activities and strategies to use before you begin to teach the unit.

- **Before, During, and After Reading (BDA):** Here you will find some generic activities and strategies to use before, during, and after students read the briefs.

 ## Unit Activities

The unit activities provide the following:

- **Student Activities:** These are specific activities that students may do after they have read the student briefs. There are a wide variety of activities for visual, logical, verbal, musical, and kinesthetic learners.

- **Key Words:** These are specific words that you may use to search the Internet to find more activities and information related specifically to the content.

- **Activity Centers:** Here you will find some ideas for the creation of activity centers that relate specifically to the unit. Not every unit is accompanied by an activity center.

- **Internet Resources:** Here you will find Internet resources that students may use with the units. Remember, however, that some of these resources may no longer be available at the time you wish to use them. Make sure that you check their availability before you incorporate them into your lesson.

 ## Student Introductions

These one-page introductions to the unit will give students a quick peek at the information they will encounter. These introductions may come in the form of flow charts, word webs, or other graphic organizers.

How This Book Is Organized *(cont.)*

 ## Unit Vocabulary

In this section, one or two pages of vocabulary words for the unit are introduced and defined.

 ## Assessments

The assessments are designed so that the same content is being tested regardless of the format of the test. Each unit in this book provides these five assessments:

- Multiple Choice
- Graphic
- Matching
- True-False
- Sentence Completion

- **Modifying the Assessments:** You may choose to modify any of these assessments by trying one of the following:

  - Give students more time to take the tests.
  - Allow students to use the briefs to help answer the questions.
  - Audio-record the tests or read the questions aloud to students.
  - Allow students to answer the questions orally.

- **Portfolio Assessment:** In addition to one of the traditional assessments, you may also use a portfolio type of assessment. Select five pieces of work (student activities) that the student has completed for the unit. Alternately, you may ask students to select five of their best pieces of work from the unit.

 ## Student Briefs

Each unit provides several student briefs. These briefs contain the core content. They are written with readability in mind, meaning that they use various fonts, bulleted lists, and spacing strategies in order to help struggling readers access the content.

Principal Stern

Mr. Jones, growing a large moustache so the students in the back of the room can see you does <u>NOT</u> count as differentiation.

It is important to remember that these briefs are only intended to provide students with a very basic, bare-bones presentation of the content. It will be up to you to provide the broader context and to fill in the details. These briefs are also designed to be used alongside your science textbook.

Generic Strategies and Activities

 Vocabulary Activities/Strategies

Provide students with a copy of the words then assign a few of the activities below:

- Draw a picture of the words.
- Scramble the words and swap with a classmate.
- Play "Hangman" with the words.
- Create a bingo game with the words.
- Write a synonym and antonym for each word.
- Act out the words.
- Write the words in a sentence.
- Snap, slap, or stomp out the syllables of the words.
- Read the words aloud.
- Teach the words to someone else.

 Building Background Activities/Strategies

Provide students with a copy of the "Student Introduction," then use a few of the strategies below:

- Go over the student introduction teaching students songs, poems, mnemonics, etc.
- Complete word webs to introduce unit concepts.
- Formulate discussion questions to activate background knowledge.
- Select a few of the discussion topics provided and allow students time to discuss.
- Have students use different color highlighter pens to mark content on the student introduction.

 Before Reading Activities/Strategies

Provide students with a copy of the "Student Brief," then use a few of the strategies below:

- Direct students' attention to the focus box.
- Show students pictures (if applicable) of the areas of study.
- Point out headings and subheadings to students.
- Have students use different color highlighter pens to highlight headings, subheadings, graphics, etc.
- Remind students that the content vocabulary is in boldfaced print.

Generic Strategies and Activities (cont.)

 During Reading Activities/Strategies

As students read each "Student Brief," use a few of the strategies below:

- Provide students with a copy of "Comprehension Cake" (page 10) so that they can record key information as they read.

- Teach students the SQR3 method:

- Use echo reading, choral reading, and/or paired reading.

- Audio-record the briefs and allow students to listen to them.

- Provide quiet areas or headphones for students who have difficulty staying focused.

- Have students use the connection sign when they encounter material that relates to something they already know. (The connection sign is simply interlacing the fingers of each hand.) Ask students to share connections.

 After Reading Activities/Strategies

After students have read the briefs, use a few of the strategies below:

- **Teach Ball:** The teach ball is a large beach ball. Have students stand. Toss the ball to a student and pose a question about the unit. If the student answers correctly, he or she tosses the ball on to another student who will answer another unit-related question. If the student doesn't know the answer, he or she says "Pass" and tosses the ball back to you. This can be repeated for several rounds.

- **Speaker's Corner:** Designate a corner of your room as "Speaker's Corner." You can put a little wooden box there on which students can stand. Ask a student to go to the speaker's corner. Ask other students to gather around. Have the student tell what he or she learned from the unit.

- **Review Comprehension Cake:** If "Comprehension Cake" was used, have students share some of the information they recorded.

Usage Tip

At the beginning of each unit, provide each student with a folder. (Preferably, the folder should have pockets, but it can simply be a piece of construction paper folded in half.) Have students write their names on their folders. As students accumulate unit material, have them collect it in their folders.

By the end of the unit, they will have a collection of unit briefs, vocabulary activities, and assessments. The content of this folder can then be used as the basis of a portfolio assessment. As a culminating activity, ask students to decorate their folders in a way that demonstrates what they have learned.

Generic Strategies and Activities (cont.)

Comprehension Cake

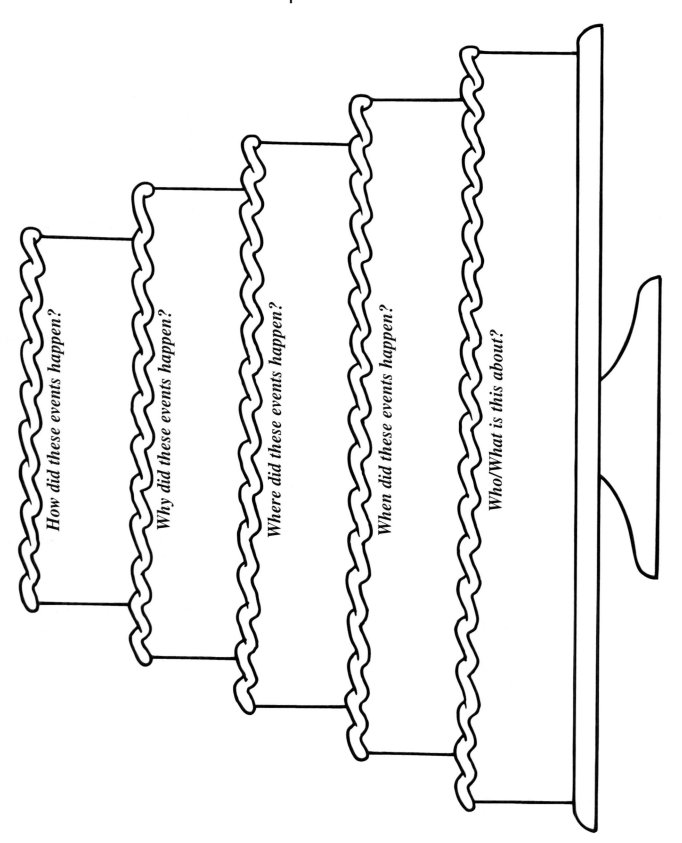

How did these events happen?

Why did these events happen?

Where did these events happen?

When did these events happen?

Who/What is this about?

McREL Content Standards

 ## Earth and Space Science

Standard 1. Understands the atmospheric processes and the water cycle

- Knows that water exists in the air in different forms and changes from one form to another through various processes

- Knows that the sun provides the light and heat necessary to maintain the temperature of the Earth

- Knows that air is a substance that surrounds us, takes up space, and moves around us as wind

Standard 2. Understands Earth's composition and structure

- Knows how features on the Earth's surface are constantly changed by a combination of slow and rapid processes

- Knows that smaller rocks come from the breakage and weathering of larger rocks and bedrock

- Knows that rock is composed of different combinations of minerals

- Knows the composition and properties of soils

 ## Life Sciences

Standard 4. Understands the principles of heredity and related concepts

- Knows that many characteristics of plants and animals are inherited from their parents and other characteristics result from an individual's interactions with the environment

Standard 5. Understands the structure and function of cells and organisms

- Knows that plants and animals progress through life cycles of birth, growth and development, and reproduction and death; and that the details of these life cycles are different for different organisms

- Knows that living organisms have distinct structures and body systems that serve specific functions in growth, survival, and reproduction

- Knows that the behavior of individual organisms is influenced by internal use (e.g., hunger) and external cues (e.g., changes in the environment) and that humans and other organisms have senses that help them to detect these cues

McREL Content Standards *(cont.)*

 Life Sciences *(cont.)*

Standard 6. Understands the relationship among organisms and their physical environment

- Knows the organization of simple food chains and food webs
- Knows that the transfer of energy (e.g., through the consumption of food) is essential to all living organisms
- Knows that an organism's patterns of behavior are related to the nature of that organism's environment
- Knows that change in the environment can have different effects on different organisms
- Knows that all organisms (including humans) cause changes in their environment, and these changes can be beneficial or detrimental

Standard 7. Understands biological evolution and the diversity of life

- Knows different ways in which living things can be grouped and the purposes of different groupings

 Physical Science

Standard 8. Understands the structure and property of matter

- Knows that matter has different states (i.e., solid, liquid, gas), and that each state has distinct physical properties; and that some common materials (such as water) can be changed from one state to another by heating or cooling
- Knows that substances can be classified by their physical and chemical properties (e.g., magnetism, conductivity, density, solubility, boiling and melting points)
- Knows that materials may be composed of parts that are too small to be seen without magnification

Standard 9. Understands the sources and properties of energy

- Knows that heat can move from one object to another by conduction and that some materials conduct heat better than others
- Knows that the pitch of a sound depends on the frequency of the vibration producing it

Classifying Living Things

Teacher Materials

 Teacher Preparation

Before you begin this unit, photocopy and distribute the following to students:

- Student Introductions (pages 16–17)
- Unit Vocabulary (pages 18–19)
- Student Briefs (pages 20–29)
- Assessments (pages 30–41)

 Key Unit Concepts

- The *cell* is the building block of all life.
- Cells have different parts that are responsible for doing different jobs.
- Plant cells and animal cells are different.
- Scientists divide all living organisms, including animals, into groups.
- In the United States and Canada, scientists usually divide and classify living organisms into six major groups (called "kingdoms").
- There are seven groups (or ranks) used to classify every animal: *Kingdom, Phylum, Class, Order, Family, Genus,* and *Species.*
- Two main groups of animal classification are *vertebrates* and *invertebrates.*
- Vertebrates are *mammals, fish, birds, reptiles,* and *amphibians.*
- The vast majority of animals are invertebrates.
- All animals have *adaptations* that help them to carry out their life processes.
- Some animal behavior is instinctual; other animal behavior is learned.
- Some traits are *inherited,* or passed from parent to offspring.

 Discussion Topics

- Have students discuss how they have changed as they have grown. How might they expect to change as they continue to get older?
- How is classification useful? In what ways do you use classification in your everyday life?
- What sorts of behaviors do humans have to learn? What behaviors are instinct? How does learning and instinct help an organism survive?

See "Generic Strategies and Activities" on pages 8 and 9 for additional strategies useful to presenting this unit.

Classifying Living Things

Activities

 Brief #1: Cells

- **Complete a Diagram:** Using a Venn diagram (see example to the right), have students compare and contrast plant and human cells.

- **Make a Model:** Have students use gelatin to make a three-dimensional model of a cell. Make sure that they include the nucleus, cell membrane, and cytoplasm.

- **Make a T-Chart:** Have students complete a T-chart (see example to the right) that lists the 10 things that are living and 10 that are non-living.

  Key Words: *Venn diagram, plant cell, human cell, cell model*

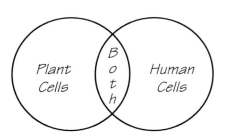

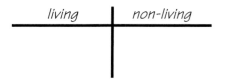

 Brief #2: The Six Kingdoms

- **Make a Postcard:** Have students select one of the six kingdoms and make a "Greetings from the Kingdom!" postcard. The postcard should contain a picture and some details about what it is like to be a member of that particular kingdom.

- **Use a Microscope:** Have students view tiny living organisms using a microscope. Ask them to describe what they see.

- **Invent an Acronym:** Have students invent an acronym or other mnemonic device to help them remember the names of the six kingdoms.

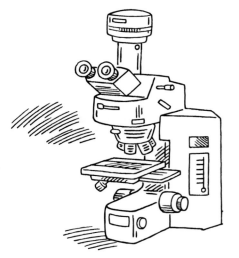

- **Create a Game:** Have students create a guessing game in which they provide the characteristics of a particular animal that classmates have to guess.

- **Write a Rhyme:** Have students select one particular invertebrate and write a rhyme or rap about its characteristics.

  Key Words: *biological classification, invertebrates*

Classifying Living Things

Activities *(cont.)*

 Brief #3: How Animals Survive

- **Invent a New Animal:** Have students invent a new animal that lives in a specific environment. Have students name and describe the animal, making sure to include specific information about how this animal is adapted to its environment.

- **Make Camouflage:** Have students pick a particular location either inside or outside of the school. Ask students to use art material and old clothes to come up with a way to change their appearance so that they blend in with the surrounding environment.

- **First-Person Narrative:** Have each student investigate one animal that is either poisonous or venomous. Have each student write a one-minute oral presentation from the point of view of that animal in which he or she describes how deadly and dangerous the animal really is!

- **Make a List:** Have students brainstorm a list of human behaviors that they think are instinctual and a list that are learned. Encourage students to debate or discuss their choices.

- **Make a Calendar:** Have students make an animal adaptations calendar. Ask students to select 12 different animals (one for each month of the year) and illustrate each animal and its particular adaptations.

  Key Words: *poisonous and venomous animals, animal adaptations*

 Internet Resources

- *http://animal.discovery.com/* — the website for the Animal Planet; includes videos, games, and current episodes of Animal Planet shows

- *http://www.kidsclick.org/midanim.html* — contains links to various animal websites that have been searched by librarians for kids; includes reading levels

- *http://www.mnh.si.edu/* — the website for the Smithsonian Museum of Natural History; includes classroom resources

Classifying Living Things

Student Introduction: Living Things Word Web

Name: _____ **Date:** _____

Directions: Use this word web to help you brainstorm characteristics of living things. What are some things that all organisms have in common? What are some examples of living things?

Living Things

Classifying Living Things

Student Introduction: Adaptations Chart

Name: _____ **Date:** _____

Directions: Complete the chart below by listing two adaptations each animal has.

Animal Adaptations

Animal	Adaptation #1	Adaptation #2
duck		
bat		
wolf		
frog		
leopard		
lizard		
spider		

Classifying Living Things

Vocabulary

1. **adaptation**—element of an animal's looks or behavior that helps it to survive

2. **amphibian**—type of cold-blooded animal that is covered in smooth skin and has both lungs and gills

3. **Animalia**—kingdom of multi-celled organisms that can move around their environment

4. **Archaea**—kingdom made up of single-celled organisms with no nucleus; often found in harsh environments, such as salt lakes and volcanic hot springs.

5. **Bacteria**—kingdom made up of single-celled organisms that have no nucleus

6. **birds**—type of warm-blooded animal that is covered in feathers and lays eggs

7. **camouflage**—adaptation which allows an animal to blend-in with its environment

8. **cell**—the smallest unit of life

9. **cell membrane**—the outermost part of the cell, which controls what substances go in and out of the cell

10. **cell wall**—part of a plant cell that helps to support the cell

11. **chloroplast**—part of the plant cell that absorbs light and makes food

12. **cytoplasm**—thick liquid that is inside of a cell

13. **exoskeleton**—hard, flexible covering of many invertebrates

14. **fish**—type of cold-blooded animal that is covered in scales and uses gills to breathe

15. **Fungi**—kingdom made up of multi-celled organisms that absorb food from both living and non-living material

16. **heredity**—the passing of traits from a parent to their offspring

Classifying Living Things

Vocabulary *(cont.)*

17. **hibernation**—animal behavior in which an animal goes to sleep for a long period of time

18. **instinct**—a behavior that an animal does not have to learn (it is inborn)

19. **invertebrate**—animal that does not have a backbone

20. **mammal**—type of warm-blooded animal that has hair or fur and gives birth to live young

21. **microscope**—a tool that is used see very, very small things

22. **migrate**—animal behavior that allows an animal to move from one place to another

23. **nucleus**—the control center of a cell

24. **organism**—something that is alive

25. **Plantae**—kingdom of multi-celled organisms that obtain most of their energy from sunlight

26. **poisonous**—an adaptation in which an animal produces a toxin that can hurt or kill predators

27. **Protist**—kingdom made up of organisms that may be both single-celled and multi-celled

28. **reptile**—cold-blooded vertebrate; often covered in scaly skin

29. **species**—most-specific group of animal classification

30. **venomous**—an adaptation that allows an animal to inject a toxin into a predator with a sting or bite

31. **vertebrate**—animal that has a backbone

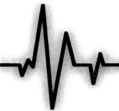

Classifying Living Things

Brief #1: Cells

Focus

All living things are made up of cells.

The world all around you is made-up of lots of different things. There are plants and animals, mountains and rivers, rocks and air. All of the things that are in the environment can be put into two different groups: living and non-living.

Living things have these features:

✓ made up of cells

✓ can get and use energy

✓ grow and change

✓ can reproduce themselves

✓ respond and adapt to their environment

Vocabulary

1. cell

2. microscope

3. cytoplasm

4. nucleus

 ### The Cell

The cell is the smallest unit of life. Sometimes people call cells the building blocks of life, because everything that it is alive, whether it is a tiger or a tulip is made up of cells. Some living things, like bacteria, are made up of only one cell, but others, like a tiger, are made up of millions of cells. You can't see cells without the help of a microscope. **A microscope is a tool that scientists use to see very, very small things.**

Even though cells are microscopic, they have different parts, and each part of the cell has a special job to do.

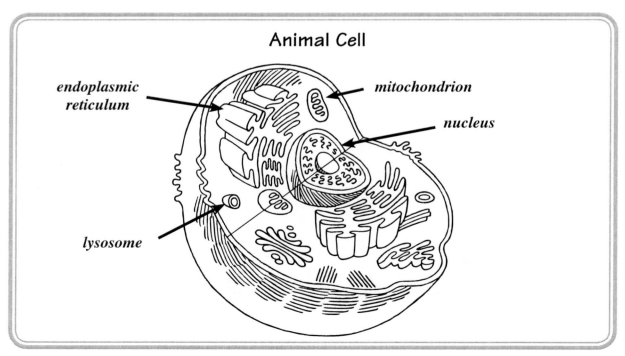

Animal Cell

endoplasmic reticulum

mitochondrion

nucleus

lysosome

Classifying Living Things

Brief #1: Cells *(cont.)*

 The Cell *(cont.)*

The cytoplasm is a kind of thick liquid that is inside of the cell. Energy is produced in the cytoplasm. **The nucleus is the control center of the cell.** It controls all of the activities of the other parts of the cell. **The outermost part of the cell is called the cell membrane.** The cell membrane controls what substances move into or out of the cell. All of these parts of the cell work together to help the cell carry out its life processes: eating, growing, and reproducing.

In plants and animals there are different types of cells. These different cells form different types of tissue. The organs in our bodies (like the stomach, liver, and heart) are made up of this tissue. But cells also make up blood, muscle, and everything else that is a part of an animal body.

> ## Vocabulary
>
> 5. cell membrane
>
> 6. chloroplast
>
> 7. cell wall

Plant cells are a little bit different from animal cells. Plants can't move around to get food like animals. That means they need a way to make their own food just by staying in one place.

If you look at a plant cell through a microscope, you see that it has a cell membrane, cytoplasm, and a nucleus. But plant cells also have something called a chloroplast. **The chloroplast is the part of the plant cell that absorbs the light the plant needs to make food.** Plants also have a cell wall. **The cell wall helps to support the cell.** Animal cells do not have cell walls.

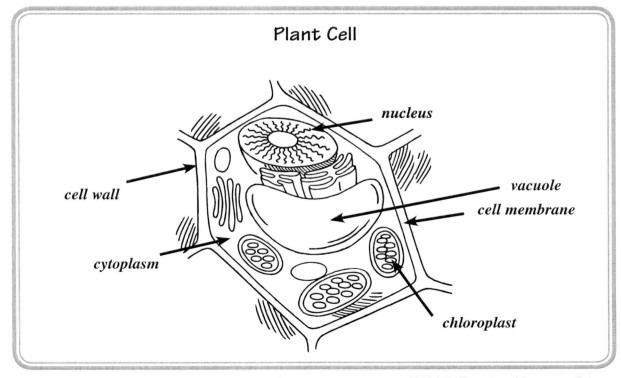

Plant Cell

Classifying Living Things

Brief #2: The Six Kingdoms

Focus

Living things are often classified into six kingdoms.

Because the world is full of millions of different types of living things, scientists put living things into groups. Scientists group living things according to what they have that is alike or different. The most basic type of group that scientists use for classifying things is called a kingdom.

There are six kingdoms:

✓ Archaea   ✓ Fungi

✓ Bacteria   ✓ Plantae

✓ Protista   ✓ Animalia

 ## Archaea

Archaea are thought to be the oldest life forms on Earth. They are made up of a single cell. But this single cell does not have a separate nucleus. It is also missing some other parts that cells usually have. Archaea are microscopic and often live in such harsh environments as hot springs, and salt lakes.

Vocabulary

1. Archaea
2. Bacteria
3. Protista
4. Fungi
5. Plantae
6. Animalia
7. organism

 ## Bacteria

Bacteria are made-up of a single cell and have no separate nucleus. Some types of bacteria can make their own food, but other types have to get food from other things. Bacteria are microscopic and live nearly everywhere on Earth, including inside of people. The human body is full of millions of bacteria. Most of it is harmless, but there are some types of bacteria that can cause a person to become ill.

 ## Protista

The Protista kingdom is very diverse. In other words, there are many differences among protists. Some protists are microscopic, but others can be seen without the help of a microscope. **Some protists are made up of a single cell, but others have many cells. All protists do have a nucleus and a simple cellular organization.** Protists usually live in water or a moist environment. Algae and amoebae are protists.

Classifying Living Things

Brief #2: The Six Kingdoms *(cont.)*

 Fungi

Fungi are living things that have many cells. Fungi cells have a nucleus. For a long time, scientists thought that fungi were plants, but now they know that they are very different from plants. Unlike most plants, fungi absorb food from other living and non-living things. Mushrooms and mold are examples of fungi. You have probably seen fungi growing on trees or on other plants. Fungus can also grow on rotten fruit—or even on people!

 Plantae

Plants are living things that are made of many cells. Plants have organs and tissues and can live on the land or in water. Plants cannot move around their environment on their own. Green plants obtain most of their energy from sunlight. Through a process called photosynthesis, these plants use sunlight to produce their food. (See page 48 for more information on photosynthesis.)

 Animalia

Animals are living things that are made of many cells. Animals have tissues, organs, and systems that are made-up of different types of cells. Animals can move around their environment. To obtain energy, most animals must eat other organisms.

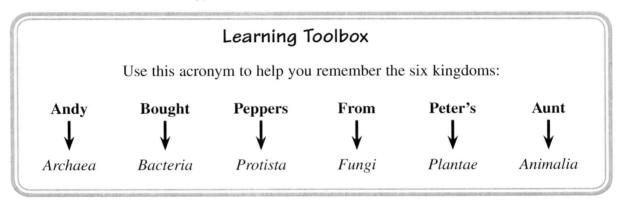

Learning Toolbox

Use this acronym to help you remember the six kingdoms:

Andy	**Bought**	**Peppers**	**From**	**Peter's**	**Aunt**
↓	↓	↓	↓	↓	↓
Archaea	*Bacteria*	*Protista*	*Fungi*	*Plantae*	*Animalia*

 Classification Within Kingdoms

The six kingdoms that are used to classify living things are large. Within each kingdom there are many different types of organisms. **An organism is something that is alive.** For example, think of all of the different plants and animals you can name. In the Bacteria, Fungi, Protista, and Archaea kingdoms there are lots of different kinds of living things, too! For this reason, scientists divide the organisms within each kingdom into even smaller and smaller groups. They group or classify the organisms according the characteristics that they have in common.

Classifying Living Things

Brief #3: Animal Classification

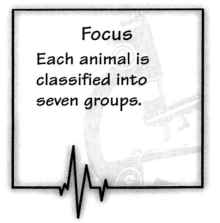

Focus

Each animal is classified into seven groups.

Within the animal kingdom, scientists use a system that classifies animals into smaller and smaller groups. The most general group of classification is called a *kingdom*. **The most specific group of animal classification is called species.** See if you can guess the animal that is being classified here.

(*Note:* In the Order, Family, Genus, and Species classifications below, the scientific name has been removed and only the description has been given.)

Guess This Animal

Kingdom ⟶ Animalia (animal)

Phylum ⟶ Chordata (animal with a backbone)

Class ⟶ Reptilia (reptile)

Order ⟶ (large, lizard-like, powerful jaws, short legs, many teeth, long snout, and hunts in water)

Family ⟶ (wider, shorter head, no teeth visible when the mouth is closed)

Genus ⟶ (lives in fresh water)

Species ⟶ (lives in the Southeastern part of the United States)

Classifying Living Things

Brief #3: Animal Classification *(cont.)*

According to the chart, you are looking for a large reptile that looks like a lizard, has short legs, a long snout, lots of teeth, and lives and hunts in fresh water in the Southeastern United States. Sound familiar? What animal could it be?

Answer: It's the *Alligator mississippiensis*—in other words, the American alligator!

Learning Toolbox

Use this acronym to help you remember the groups of animal classification:

King	**Phillip**	**Can**	**Only**	**Find**	**Green**	**Slippers**
↓	↓	↓	↓	↓	↓	↓
Kingdom	*Phylum*	*Class*	*Order*	*Family*	*Genus*	*Species*

 ### Vertebrates and Invertebrates

The animal kingdom is full of thousands of different kinds of animals. Some are as big as whales, others are as tiny as fleas. But all of these animals can be grouped according to some very simple characteristics.

Two main groups of animals are vertebrates and invertebrates. **Vertebrates are animals that have a spine or a backbone.** For example, snakes, elephants, birds, and fish are all vertebrates. **Invertebrates are animals that don't have a spine or backbone.** For example, worms, insects, jellyfish, lobsters, and spiders are all invertebrates.

Vocabulary

1. species
2. vertebrates
3. invertebrates
4. mammals
5. fish
6. birds
7. amphibians
8. reptiles
9. exoskeleton

Classifying Living Things

Brief #3: Animal Classification *(cont.)*

 Differences Among Vertebrates

Vertebrates are divided up into even smaller groups. **Mammals are vertebrates that have skin, hair, or fur.** They have lungs and are warm-blooded. Mammals can control their body temperatures and usually give birth to live young.

Fish are vertebrates that are usually covered in scales. Instead of breathing with lungs, they have gills. They are cold-blooded and lay eggs.

Birds are vertebrates that are usually covered in feathers. They breathe with lungs and are warm-blooded. They usually lay eggs.

Amphibians are vertebrates that are usually covered in smooth skin. They may have both lungs and gills, because they can live on the land and in the water. They are cold-blooded and lay eggs.

Reptiles are vertebrates that are usually covered in scaly skin. They have lungs and usually live on the land. They are cold-blooded. Most of them lay eggs, but there are some reptiles that give birth to live young.

Vertebrates

mammals	whales, cats, bats, humans
fish	sharks, sea horses, tuna, eels
birds	eagles, sea gulls, parrots, pigeons
amphibians	frogs, toads, salamanders
reptiles	snakes, lizards, turtles

 Differences Among Invertebrates

There are more invertebrates than vertebrates. In fact, about 98% of all of the animals that exist are invertebrates. Some invertebrates, like worms, have very soft bodies that have no protections. Others, like lobsters, have hard shells that protect their soft bodies. Spiders have something called an exoskeleton. **An exoskeleton is a hard but flexible outer skin that protects an animal's body.**

The largest group of animals on Earth is a group of invertebrates called arthropods. Spiders and crabs are examples of arthropods. They have jointed legs and an exoskeleton.

Another large group of invertebrates are sponges. Sponges look like plants, but they

Invertebrates

Annelida	segmented worms, earthworms
Arthropoda	spiders, crabs, wasps
Cnidaria	jellyfish, coral
Mollusca	snails, squid, oysters
Porifera	sponges

are really animals. They attach themselves permanently to something in the water and can carry out their life processes from that one location.

Classifying Living Things

Brief #4: How Animals Survive

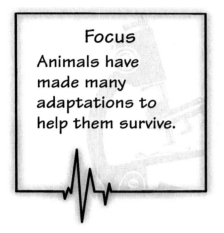

Focus

Animals have made many adaptations to help them survive.

All animals, whether they are vertebrates or invertebrates, feature adaptations that help them to get what they need to survive. All animals have such needs as food, oxygen, water, and shelter. These things help animals carry out their life processes. **An animal's life processes are birth, growth, and reproduction.**

 Adaptations

An animal adaptation is something about the animal's body or behavior that helps it to get what it needs to survive. Think about all of the animals that you know. What is it about their bodies that helps them to get what they need? Do they blend into the environment?

What about the way they act? Can they swim fast or fly high? And how does blending in or being fast help them to survive? The feathers of a bird help them to fly. If you look carefully at a bird's beak you will see that it is very useful for getting the food that it eats. Some birds eat seeds. Their beak is good for cracking the seeds open. Other birds hunt for fish. These birds have long, thin beaks that help them spear the fish in the water. The feathers of a bird help to keep them warm and waterproof. The webbed feet of many birds help them to swim well and walk around in mud.

Vocabulary

1. adaptation
2. camouflage
3. poisonous
4. venomous
5. instinct
6. migrate
7. hibernate
8. heredity

But what about mammals? They feature many adaptations, too. Think about a camel. There are camels that have one hump and camels that have two humps. Many people think that camels carry water in those humps, but that is not true: inside those humps is a store of fatty tissue. Camels can turn that fatty tissue into water, which is useful if you live in a desert! Camels also have two rows of long, thick eyelashes. This helps them to protect their eyes from sandstorms that happen in the desert.

Classifying Living Things

Brief #4: How Animals Survive *(cont.)*

 ### Protection

All animals live in an environment where there can be danger. Think about your environment. How do you keep yourself safe from danger? Animals have many ways to keep themselves safe. One of the things that some of them can do is to use camouflage. *Camouflage* **means being able to blend in or change the way you look.**

Some animals are naturally camouflaged to blend in with their environment. A polar bear is one example. Polar bears are white so they can blend in with the white snow. Lions also blend in this way with their environments. Fish that live among coral are often brightly colored so that they are almost impossible to detect among the brightly colored coral. Blending in with your environment is very useful. If a predator can't see you, then it can't eat you!

There are many different ways that animals can use their appearance to protect themselves. Some animals—like certain frogs, lizards, and fish—can actually change their color so that their predators can't find them. Other animals have certain designs on their bodies or shapes that can help to keep them safe. For example, there are insects that are shaped like leaves. The bodies of other insects may contain patterns that looks like the eyes of a much larger animal.

 ### Defenses

An animal's appearance is one way it can keep itself safe. Another way is the use of poison. Many animals, like snakes, frogs, and insects, are either venomous or poisonous. **If an animal is poisonous, there is a toxic substance on its skin. If you touch it or try to eat it, you will take in the poison. If an animal is venomous, its bite or sting can inject a toxic substance into you.**

> ### Fast Fact
>
> The bite of the Sydney funnel web spider can kill a person in less then 15 minutes.

Classifying Living Things

Brief #4: How Animals Survive *(cont.)*

 Instinct and Learning

All animals are born with certain instincts. **An instinct is a helpful behavior an organism has that it doesn't have to learn.** For instance, if a person sees an object moving quickly in the direction of his or her face, that person will automatically shut his or her eyes.

Migration is an animal behavior that is an instinct. **Many animals migrate or move from one place to another during different times of the year.** Many types of birds migrate from cold places to warm places, and whales migrate in the oceans to safe places where they can breed. Migration is an instinct because animals are born knowing how to do it.

Hibernation is an animal behavior in which the animal goes to sleep for several months. Hibernation is also an instinct. Hibernation happens during the winter months. During hibernation, an animal's body temperature drops and its heart rate slows down. Hibernation helps animals to conserve energy during cold months. Bears, bats, and some reptiles and amphibians hibernate.

An animal's behavior is not all instinct. Many animals inherit the ability to learn from their parents. **Heredity is when an animal parent passes down traits to its offspring.** For example, a human baby is not born knowing how to read. But its parents passed down to them the ability to learn how to read.

Many animals learn how to do lots of things from their parents. Birds learn how to fly from their parents, tigers and lions learn to hunt, and elephants learn to recognize the calls of their herd.

Classifying Living Things

Multiple-Choice Assessment

Name: _____ **Date:** _____

Directions: Read each question carefully. Fill in the correct answer circle.

1. Which of the following is living?

   Ⓐ rock

   Ⓑ duck

   Ⓒ water

   Ⓓ soil

2. What is the smallest unit of life?

   Ⓐ molecule

   Ⓑ atom

   Ⓒ cell

   Ⓓ membrane

3. What must you use to see a cell?

   Ⓐ telescope

   Ⓑ x-ray machine

   Ⓒ magnifying glass

   Ⓓ microscope

4. What part of the cell is in control?

   Ⓐ nucleus

   Ⓑ cytoplasm

   Ⓒ chloroplast

   Ⓓ cell wall

5. What does a plant cell have that a human cell does not have?

   Ⓐ nucleus

   Ⓑ chloroplast

   Ⓒ cell membrane

   Ⓓ cytoplasm

Classifying Living Things

Multiple-Choice Assessment *(cont.)*

6. Into how many kingdoms are living organisms usually classified by scientists in the United States and Canada?

   Ⓐ 6

   Ⓑ 5

   Ⓒ 9

   Ⓓ 12

---

7. Which of the following is not a kingdom?

   Ⓐ Protista

   Ⓑ Fungi

   Ⓒ Plantae

   Ⓓ Mammalia

---

8. Archaea and bacteria are made-up of

   Ⓐ many-cells

   Ⓑ one cell

   Ⓒ ten cells

   Ⓓ many cells with no nucleus

---

9. How are plants and fungi different?

   Ⓐ Plants absorb nutrients from rocks, but fungi don't.

   Ⓑ Fungi have more cells than plants.

   Ⓒ Plants get most of their energy from sunlight, but fungi can't.

   Ⓓ Fungi can live in below freezing temperatures, but plants can't.

---

10. Why must plants use sunlight to get most of their energy?

   Ⓐ Because they can't move around to get food for energy.

   Ⓑ Because they spend all of their time outside.

   Ⓒ Because they need specialized food.

   Ⓓ none of these

Classifying Living Things

Multiple-Choice Assessment *(cont.)*

11. What is the most specific group of animal classification?

Ⓐ kingdom

Ⓑ phylum

Ⓒ genus

Ⓓ species

12. What is a vertebrate?

Ⓐ animal with no backbone

Ⓑ animal with segmented legs

Ⓒ animal with a backbone

Ⓓ animal with an exoskeleton

13. Which of the following is an invertebrate?

Ⓐ monkey

Ⓑ spider

Ⓒ frog

Ⓓ snake

14. What kind of covering do mammals have?

Ⓐ scales and skin

Ⓑ skin, fur, or hair

Ⓒ scales

Ⓓ feathers

15. Where would you find an exoskeleton?

Ⓐ on the outside of the body

Ⓑ on the inside of the body

Ⓒ in the gills

Ⓓ in the cell

Classifying Living Things

Multiple-Choice Assessment *(cont.)*

16. Blending in is called

    Ⓐ mimicry.

    Ⓑ camouflage.

    Ⓒ instinct.

    Ⓓ all of these.

---

17. An instinct is

    Ⓐ a learned behavior.

    Ⓑ a defensive behavior.

    Ⓒ a migrating behavior.

    Ⓓ a behavior an organism is born with.

---

18. How does hibernation help an animal survive?

    Ⓐ The animal conserves energy.

    Ⓑ The animal hides from prey.

    Ⓒ The animal gets good rest.

    Ⓓ The animal learns to hunt.

---

19. Inherited abilities are passed from

    Ⓐ offspring to parents.

    Ⓑ parents to offspring.

    Ⓒ offspring to offspring.

    Ⓓ vertebrates to invertebrates.

---

20. What are life processes?

    Ⓐ birth and death

    Ⓑ birth, growth, and reproduction

    Ⓒ growth, learning, and hibernation

    Ⓓ migration, instinct, and reproduction

Classifying Living Things

Sentence-Completion Assessment

Name: _____ **Date:** _____

Directions: Read each statement. Fill in the word or words that best complete the sentence.

1. A rock is an example of something that is _____ .

2. The smallest unit of life is called a _____ .

3. In order to see a cell, you must use a _____ .

4. The _____ is known as the brain of the cell.

5. The chloroplast is located in a _____ cell.

6. In the U.S. and Canada, scientists usually classify living organisms into _____ kingdoms.

7. The kingdoms are _____, _____,

    Protista, _____, _____, and Animalia.

8. Bacteria are _____-celled.

9. Mold is classified in the _____ kingdom.

10. _____ use sunlight to get their food because they can't move around.

Classifying Living Things

Sentence-Completion Assessment *(cont.)*

11. _____ is the most specific group of animal classification.

12. An animal with a _____ is called a vertebrate.

13. An animal without a backbone is called an _____ .

14. _____ usually have fur or hair.

15. An _____ is the hard, flexible covering of a spider.

16. The ability of an animal to blend in with its environment is called

_____ .

17. An _____ is a behavior that an animal is born with.

18. During _____ , an animal conserves energy.

19. Animals get inherited traits from their _____

20. Birth, growth, and reproduction are called _____ .

Classifying Living Things

True-False Assessment

Name: _____ **Date:** _____

Directions: Read each statement carefully. If the statement is true, put a **T** on the line provided. If the statement is false, put an **F** on the line provided.

_____ **1.** A rock is considered living.

_____ **2.** A cell is the smallest unit of life.

_____ **3.** A microscope is not needed to see a cell.

_____ **4.** The cell membrane is kind of like the control center of the cell.

_____ **5.** Plant cells have chloroplasts.

_____ **6.** Living organisms are often classified into six kingdoms.

_____ **7.** Protists are not a kingdom.

_____ **8.** Archaea and bacteria are single-celled.

_____ **9.** Most plants can use sunlight to produce their own food.

_____ **10.** Most fungi can use sunlight to produce their own food.

_____ **11.** Genus is the most specific group of animal classification.

_____ **12.** A vertebrate has a backbone.

(GO)

Classifying Living Things

True-False Assessment *(cont.)*

_____ **13.** An invertebrate has a backbone.

_____ **14.** Mammals have fur or hair.

_____ **15.** An exoskeleton is located on the outside of the body.

_____ **16.** Camouflage is blending in.

_____ **17.** An instinct must be learned.

_____ **18.** During hibernation animals hunt.

_____ **19.** Inherited traits are passed from parents to offspring.

_____ **20.** Life processes are birth, growth, and reproduction.

Classifying Living Things

Matching Assessment

Name: _____ **Date:** _____

Directions: Read the items in both lists below and on page 39 carefully. Choose an item from List B that best matches an item from List A. Write the corresponding letter from List B on the line. You will have some left over.

List A	List B
_____ 1. non-living	A. smallest unit of life
_____ 2. cell	B. genus
_____ 3. microscope	C. rock
_____ 4. nucleus	D. tool for seeing cells
_____ 5. chloroplast	E. main source of energy for plants
_____ 6. usual number of kingdoms	F. six
_____ 7. amphibian	G. conserves energy
_____ 8. single-celled organisms	H. plant cells only
_____ 9. hibernation	I. control center of cell
_____ 10. sunlight	J. bacteria
_____ 11. species	K. salamander
_____ 12. vertebrate	L. outside of body

(GO)

Classifying Living Things

Matching Assessment *(cont.)*

List A	List B
_____ **13.** invertebrate	**M.** helpful, automatic behavior
_____ **14.** fur and hair	**N.** no backbone
_____ **15.** location of exoskeleton	**O.** backbone
_____ **16.** blending in	**P.** venomous
_____ **17.** instinct	**Q.** camouflage
_____ **18.** fungi	**R.** passed to offspring
_____ **19.** inherited traits	**S.** smallest group of classification
_____ **20.** life processes	**T.** lives off other things
	U. birth, growth, reproduction
	V. mammal coverings

STOP

Classifying Living Things

Graphic Assessment

Name: _____ **Date:** _____

Directions: Look carefully at the diagram of the cell below. Locate and label the following cell parts: *cell wall, nucleus, cytoplasm, cell membrane.*

GO

Classifying Living Things

Graphic Assessment *(cont.)*

Directions: Complete the chart below by adding as much detail as possible.

Types of Vertebrates

Group	Characteristics	Examples
fish		
	skin, fur, or hair	
		frog, toad
bird		
	cold-blooded, has lungs	

Directions: Name five animals that are invertebrates.

1. _____

2. _____

3. _____

4. _____

5. _____

Plants

Teacher Materials

 Teacher Preparation

Before you begin this unit, photocopy and distribute the following to students:

- Student Introductions (pages 45–46)
- Unit Vocabulary (page 47)
- Student Briefs (pages 48–53)
- Assessments (pages 54–65)

 Key Unit Concepts

- Plants use *photosynthesis* to produce energy.
- *Chlorophyll* makes plants green.
- There are *nonvascular* and *vascular* plants.
- The various parts of flowers are adaptations that help them reproduce.
- *Pollination* occurs when pollen is transferred from the *stamens* to the *pistil*.
- *Fertilization* occurs when sperm cells combine with eggs.
- Animals, wind, and water help pollination, fertilization, and *seed dispersal*.
- Different types of plants have different ways in which they reproduce.

 Discussion Topics

- Compare and contrast plants and animals. How are they alike? How are they different?
- What does the word *interdependence* mean? How do you think plants and animals are interdependent?

> See "Generic Strategies and Activities" on pages 8 and 9 for additional strategies useful to presenting this unit.

Plants

Activities

 Brief #1: How Plants Obtain Energy

- **Make a Diagram:** Have students make a diagram that shows how the process of photosynthesis works.

- **Perform an Experiment:** Have students conduct an experiment to see what happens when a plant is deprived of the ability to make chemical energy. Use two houseplants. Place them side-by-side on a windowsill. Place a paper bag over one. Do not water that plant. Care for the other plant as usual. Have students record their observations over a one-week period of time.

- **Research and Report:** Have students research why the leaves on some trees in some places turn different colors in the autumn. Ask them to write a short paragraph that explains the process.

   Key Word: *photosynthesis*

 Brief #2: Types of Plants

- **Identify Leaves:** Using a leaf identification book or website, have students collect a variety of different kinds of leaves from around the school and try to identify them.

- **Create a T-Chart:** Make a T-chart that lists at least 10 varieties of vascular and nonvascular plants.

- **Create Leaf Rubbings:** Have students create a collection of a variety of leaves from the area. Lay a leaf on a flat surface. Place a piece of tracing paper over the leaf. Gently rub over the tracing paper with a pencil until the leaf shows through the tracing paper. Have students label the types of leaves they have traced.

   Key Words: *types of vascular and nonvascular plants*

Plants

Activities *(cont.)*

 Brief #3: How Plants Reproduce

- **Grow and Observe:** Have students grow an amaryllis plant in the classroom. The various parts of the flower (pistil, stamens, etc.) are quite visible with this plant; however, students should also use a magnifying lens to get a good look at the reproductive organs of the plant.

- **Make a Poster:** Have students bring in several different pieces of fruit (for example, apples, pears, peaches, oranges). Ask the students to remove the seeds and observe them under a microscope. On a large piece of poster board, have students paste the seeds of each fruit on the board and write a few lines to describe the seed and the fruit from which it comes.

- **Research and Narrate:** Have students research several insect pollinators. Ask them to write a short monologue in which they tell what their everyday lives are like as pollinators. Have students perform the monologue for the class.

    Key Words: *amaryllis plant, pollinator*

 Internet Resources

- *http://www.picadome.fcps.net/lab/currl/plants/default.htm* — well-researched website about plants; includes printable worksheets and time-lapse videos of blooming flowers

Plants

Student Introduction: Plants Word Web

Name: _____   **Date:** _____

Directions: Use this word web to help you brainstorm characteristics of plants. What are some things that all plants have in common? What are the names of the different plant parts?

Plants

Plants

Student Introduction: Photosynthesis

Name: _____ **Date:** _____

Directions: This is an illustration of photosynthesis. Photosynthesis is the process that plants use in order to create chemical energy. Make each part of this illustration a different color.

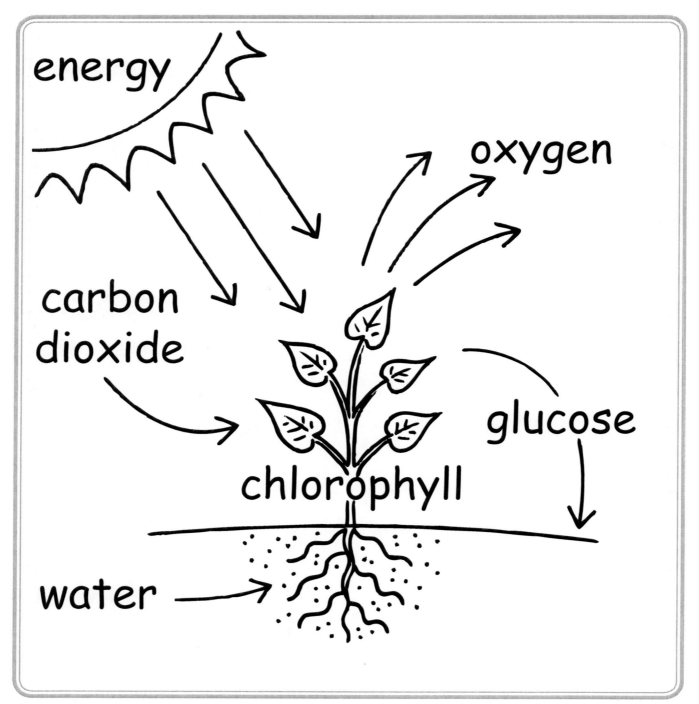

energy

oxygen

carbon dioxide

glucose

chlorophyll

water

Plants

Vocabulary

1. **anthers**—the tips of the stamens where the sperm cells are located

2. **chlorophyll**—the substance inside of the chloroplasts that make the plants green

3. **conifers**—cone-producing plants

4. **fertilization**—the combining of sperm cells and eggs

5. **leaves**—the part of vascular plants that gathers carbon dioxide

6. **nectar**—sweet liquid produced by flowers

7. **nonvascular plants**—plants that distribute water and nutrients from cell to cell

8. **petal**—the part of a flower that protects the seeds

9. **photosynthesis**—the process plants use to make food

10. **pistil**—the female, egg-producing part of the flower

11. **pollination**—the transfer of pollen from the stamens to the pistil

12. **roots**—the part of a vascular plant that draws water and nutrients from the grounds

13. **seed dispersal**—the process whereby seeds are moved from place to place

14. **sepals**—small, green leaves beneath the flower that help to protect it

15. **stamens**—the male, sperm-cell-producing part of the flower

16. **stems**—the part of a vascular plant that transports water and nutrients from the roots to the leaves

17. **spores**—reproduction cells located on the back of the leaves of ferns

18. **vascular plants**—plants that distribute water and nutrients through stems, roots, and leaves

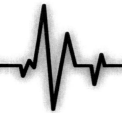

Plants

Brief #1: How Plants Obtain Energy

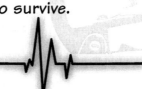

Focus

Plants use the process of photosynthesis to make the chemical energy they need to survive.

All organisms need energy in order to survive. Every organism has a way in which it can get energy. Animals graze or hunt, people grow food or go to the supermarket, etc. But plants cannot move around. They are kept in one place by their roots. Because plants can't graze or hunt, they have another method for getting the energy they need. **The process plants use to produce chemical energy is called photosynthesis.**

You learned that plant cells are different from the cells of animals. Plant cells have something called chloroplasts. It is the chloroplasts that make photosynthesis possible.

Vocabulary

1. photosynthesis
2. chlorophyll

 ### How Photosynthesis Works

You know that plants have leaves and roots. The leaves and the roots of the plants have important jobs to do. The leaves absorb (take in) carbon dioxide from the environment. The plants absorb water through their roots, which are buried in the ground. The water travels up the plants through their stems.

When sunlight shines on its leaves, a plant changes the water and the carbon dioxide into sugar. It is this sugar that the plant uses as food. The sugar is delivered to all of the parts of the plant through small tubes and through the plant's stem. Sugar that the plant doesn't use right away is stored in the stem and in the leaves.

The process of photosynthesis also produces oxygen. But plants don't use oxygen, so it is released into the environment. This is lucky for us! Animals need oxygen to survive.

 ### Why Plants Are Green

Inside of all plants cells there are chloroplasts. Inside of those chloroplasts is a green substance called chlorophyll. **It is the chlorophyll in plant cells that captures the energy from sunlight.** During the process of photosynthesis, plants change the energy from the sunlight into the sugar that they use as energy.

Plants

Brief #2: Types of Plants

Focus
Plants can be vascular or nonvascular.

There are two main classifications of plants. Plants can be either vascular or nonvascular. **A vascular plant is a plant that has leaves, stems, and roots.** Water and nutrients move through all of these plant parts to make sure that the plant gets what it needs to carry out its life processes.

Trees are vascular plants. A tree absorbs water from the ground through its root system. The water travels up through its trunk and then out to the branches and to the leaves.

Trees can be very large, of course, but vascular plants can come in all shapes and sizes. Grass, bushes, shrubs, and flowers are all vascular plants.

Parts of Vascular Plants

All vascular plants, no matter their size or what they look like, have some things in common. All vascular plants have leaves. **The leaves of a vascular plant absorb energy from sunlight and turn that energy into food.**

Leaves come in all shapes and sizes. The way a leaf looks and how it is arranged on a stem depends on where the tree is located. For example, the trees located nearer to the forest floor in a rainforest usually have large leaves. That's because these trees live in a shady environment and need to gather as much sunlight as possible.

All vascular plants also have stems. Stems that are very large are called trunks, but they all do the same job: **the stems of vascular plants transport water and nutrients from the roots to the branches and leaves.** The stem of a plant also helps to support the plant and hold the leaves in the best position to gather the energy from the sunlight.

Vocabulary

1. vascular plants
2. leaves
3. stems
4. roots
5. nonvascular plants

Learning Toolbox

Sung to the tune of "Three Blind Mice":

Vas-cu-lar plants have roots,

Vas-cu-lar plants have roots,

The roots and the leaves and the stems of the plants

Take water and nutrients round to the plants

So they can be home to the birds and the ants

Those plants with roots.

Plants

Brief #2: Types of Plants *(cont.)*

 Parts of Vascular Plants *(cont.)*

Vascular plants also have roots. **The roots of vascular plants are buried in the ground. The job of the roots is to absorb water and nutrients from the ground and transport them to the stems of the plants.**

Vascular plants may have different kinds of root systems. A *tap root system* has a single large root that grows straight down into the soil. If you look closely at a tap root you will see lots of tiny hairs that grown on the root. These tiny hairs also absorb water and nutrients. A *fibrous-root system* has a collection of many tiny roots that grow in lots of different directions.

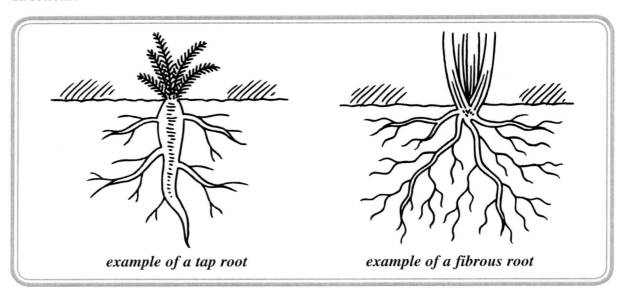

example of a tap root   *example of a fibrous root*

 Nonvascular Plants

Nonvascular plants don't have leaves, stems, or roots. But they, too, make their own chemical energy, so they have a different way of absorbing and transporting water and nutrients. **Nonvascular plants are plants that absorb water from their environment and pass it from cell to cell.** Nonvascular plants usually always grow in moist places, very close to the ground.

The most common type of nonvascular plant is moss. You may have seen moss growing on the rocks near rivers or creeks. The moss grows so tightly together it almost looks like a single plant. Hornworts and liverworts are other types of nonvascular plants.

> **Fast Fact**
>
> There are over 10,000 different species of moss.

Plants

Brief #3: How Plants Reproduce

One of the life processes of any type of living organism is the ability to reproduce. *Reproduction* means to make more of your species. Human beings have babies, dogs have pups, and cats have kittens. Plants also reproduce.

 Flowers and Cones

For us, flowers are something beautiful to look at and to smell. But flowers have a very important job. If it were not for flowers, plants would not be able to reproduce!

If you look carefully at a flower, you will see that it has several different parts. Each part has a specific job to do. The petals of a flower can be different shapes and colors.

Think of some of the flowers you know, like roses, daisies, and tulips. The petals of each of these flowers are very different.

The petals of a flower help to protect the seeds. Also, the color and smell of the flowers attracts birds, bees, and other animals that are needed to help the plants reproduce.

Beneath the flowers you will see small green leaves. These tiny leaves are called sepals. **Sepals help to protect the flowers as it begins to bloom.** They cover the bud of the flower.

In the very center of a flower you will spot the pistil. **The pistil is the female part of the flower.** That means that it is the part of the flower that produces egg cells. Surrounding the pistil are the stamens. **The stamens are the male parts of the flower. Pollen is produced on the tips of the stamens, which are called anthers.** The flower's seed is formed when the sperm cells on the anthers combine with the eggs in the pistil.

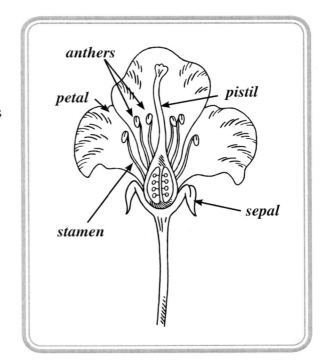

There are other plants that make seeds, but instead of having flowers, they have cones. These plants are called conifers. A pine tree is an example of a conifer. Conifers grow two different kinds of cones. One cone makes the pollen, while the other makes the seeds. These types of plants are called *evergreen* because their leaves or needles don't fall off during the winter.

Plants

Brief #3: How Plants Reproduce *(cont.)*

 ### Pollination

The seeds of plants are formed by a process called pollination. **During pollination, the pollen is transferred from the stamens to the pistil.** But how does the pollen get from plant to plant? Unlike animals, plants can't move around. Instead, they have to rely on other things to help spread the pollen around the environment and fertilize other plants.

During certain times of the year, you will see birds, bees, butterflies, and other types of animals hovering above the flowers in your garden. They are attracted to nectar. **Nectar is a kind of sweet liquid that flowers produce.** Nectar is also the raw material from which honey is produced. Birds, bees, and other insects love the taste of nectar, so once flowers are in bloom, they spend their time flying from one flower to the next in search of this sweet drink.

As these animals drink the nectar from the flowers, the pollen from the stamens rubs off onto their bodies. When they fly to another flower, this pollen is deposited on the pistil of another flower.

Vocabulary
1. petal
2. sepals
3. pistil
4. stamens
5. anthers
6. conifers
7. pollination
8. nectar
9. fertilization
10. seed dispersal
11. spores

 ### Fertilization

Once the flower has been pollinated, a tube grows down the pistil to the ovary, which is located at the bottom. **Sperm cells fall down this tube and combine with the plant's egg. This is called fertilization.**

There are lots of plants that are fertilized in a different way. Trees and grass depend on the wind to spread pollen from one tree to another. Perhaps in the spring you have noticed a thin covering of a greenish dust on the cars. Maybe you have seen pollen being blown from tree to tree. Many people have bad allergies during the time when grass and trees are pollinating.

Fast Fact

Pollen count is a measurement of how many grains of pollen there are in the air.

After a plant is fertilized, the petals and the stamens dry up and fall off the plants. The fertilized eggs grow into seeds. The type of seed the plants produce depends on the kind of plant that it is. Some seeds are protected by fruit, like apples and peaches. The seeds of the flowerings plants are what grow into new plants.

Plants

Brief #3: How Plants Reproduce *(cont.)*

 ### Seed Dispersal

Just as animals and wind help plants to make seeds, they also help plants to spread their seeds around the environment. You will often see bunches of the same type of plants together. That's because the seeds of the plants have fallen to the ground around the parent plants. Many seeds can take root this way. But this isn't always the best place for a seed to begin its life. Just imagine a tiny maple tree trying to grow beneath the shade and amongst the roots of a maple tree that is 50 years old! The tiny seed wouldn't have a very good chance of survival.

One way that seeds get from place to place is on the water. Plants that grow near water drop their seeds into rivers, lakes, and creeks. The currents of the water take the seeds far away from where they originally began, and some plants take root in these new locations.

Another way that seeds travel from one place to another is through the wind. Seeds on the ground are swept up in wind currents and deposited in new places.

A third way in which seeds move through the environment is by being carried to new places by animals. Have you ever returned from a hike in the woods and discovered that you had seeds in your hair or stuck to your socks? If so, then you have helped with seed dispersal. **Seed dispersal is the process by which seeds are moved from one place to another.** Many different kinds of seeds attach themselves to the bodies of such animals as bats, squirrels, and birds. As these animals move through the environment, the seeds are moved from place to place.

 ### Spores

Not all plants produce flowers or cones. That means that they don't produce seeds, either. But they must have a way in which to reproduce. That's where spores come into the picture. Ferns and mosses have tiny cells on the backside of their leaves. They look like small dots. **These small cells are spores.** If the spores land on wet ground and all of the other conditions are right, the spores can germinate. When a seed or a spore germinates, it has taken root and is beginning to grow.

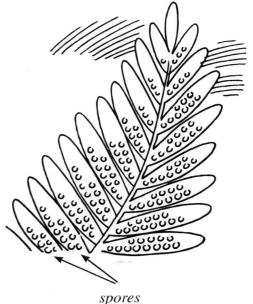

spores

Plants

Multiple-Choice Assessment

Name: _____   **Date:** _____

Directions: Read each question carefully. Fill in the correct answer circle.

1. How do plants make chemical energy?

   Ⓐ osmosis

   Ⓑ photosynthesis

   Ⓒ germination

   Ⓓ pollination

2. What substance do the leaves of plants take in to help them make chemical energy?

   Ⓐ oxygen

   Ⓑ carbon

   Ⓒ carbon dioxide

   Ⓓ nitrogen

3. Which of the following is the type of fuel that plants make?

   Ⓐ sugar

   Ⓑ starch

   Ⓒ spores

   Ⓓ pollen

4. Which of the following is a by-product of photosynthesis?

   Ⓐ carbon dioxide

   Ⓑ carbon monoxide

   Ⓒ hydrogen

   Ⓓ oxygen

5. Why are plants green?

   Ⓐ They contain chloroform.

   Ⓑ They contain chloroplasts.

   Ⓒ The sun makes them green.

   Ⓓ They contain chlorophyll.

Plants

Multiple-Choice Assessment *(cont.)*

6. What energy do plants mostly use to produce chemical energy?

Ⓐ oxygen

Ⓑ sunlight

Ⓒ wind energy

Ⓓ cells

---

7. If a plant is vascular, what does it have?

Ⓐ cones and flowers

Ⓑ moss

Ⓒ stems, roots, and leaves

Ⓓ all of these

---

8. How does a liverwort distribute nutrients around the plant?

Ⓐ through veins

Ⓑ through shallow roots

Ⓒ from cell to cell

Ⓓ from stem to cell

---

9. How is a tap root different from a fibrous root?

Ⓐ A tap root is deep; a fibrous root is shallow.

Ⓑ A fibrous root grows directly down; a tap rot grows in many directions.

Ⓒ A tap root grows straight down; a fibrous root grows in many directions.

Ⓓ Tap roots and fibrous roots are single-celled.

---

10. Liverworts and hornworts are both

Ⓐ vascular plants.

Ⓑ nonvascular plants.

Ⓒ conifers.

Ⓓ mosses.

Plants

Multiple-Choice Assessment *(cont.)*

11. What is the job of a petal?

Ⓐ to look beautiful

Ⓑ to smell nice

Ⓒ to protect the seeds

Ⓓ to distribute the seeds

---

12. Where would you find the sepals?

Ⓐ in the root

Ⓑ on top of the petal

Ⓒ inside of the stamens

Ⓓ beneath the petal

---

13. Which part of the flower is female?

Ⓐ the pistil

Ⓑ the stamens

Ⓒ the sepals

Ⓓ the ovary

---

14. Where is the pollen produced?

Ⓐ in the pistil

Ⓑ in the stamens

Ⓒ conifer

Ⓓ none of these

---

15. What important substance is located on the anthers?

Ⓐ spores

Ⓑ cells

Ⓒ sperm cells

Ⓓ nectar

Plants

Multiple-Choice Assessment *(cont.)*

16. What does a conifer have?

Ⓐ petals

Ⓑ spores

Ⓒ cones

Ⓓ honey

---

17. Pollination is the transfer of pollen from

Ⓐ the petals to the pistil.

Ⓑ the stamens to the pistil.

Ⓒ the pistil to the nectar.

Ⓓ the stamens to the spores.

---

18. A sweet substance produced by flowers is called

Ⓐ nectar.

Ⓑ honey.

Ⓒ pollen.

Ⓓ sap.

---

19. Fertilization is when

Ⓐ pollen is transferred from the stamens to the pistil.

Ⓑ seeds geminate in the ground.

Ⓒ sperm cells combine with the plant's egg.

Ⓓ the plant's egg combines with the seeds.

---

20. Where might you find a spore?

Ⓐ on the petal of a fern.

Ⓑ on the stamen of a fern.

Ⓒ on the pistil of a fern.

Ⓓ on the back of the leaf of a fern.

Plants

Sentence-Completion Assessment

Name: _____ **Date:** _____

Directions: Read each statement. Fill in the word or words that best complete the sentence.

1. Plants use the process of _____ to make chemical energy.

2. The leaves of plants absorb _____ in order to help them

    produce chemical energy.

3. The food that plants make is _____ .

4. _____ is a by-product of photosynthesis.

5. The _____ in plants is what makes them green.

6. Energy from _____ helps plants to produce food.

7. Vascular plants have stems, _____ and _____ .

8. _____ plants distribute water and nutrients from cell

    to _____ .

9. A _____ root grows directly down into the ground.

10. Liverworts and hornworts are both _____ plants.

Plants

Sentence-Completion Assessment *(cont.)*

11. The _____ of a flower helps to protect the seeds.

12. The tiny leaves beneath flowers are called _____ .

13. The female part of the flower is called the _____ .

14. Pollen is produced in the flower's _____ .

15. The flower's sperm cells are located on the _____ .

16. Instead of flowers, conifers have _____ .

17. During pollination, pollen is transferred from the _____

    to the _____ .

18. The sweet substance produced by flowers is called _____ .

19. The fertilization of a flower occurs when the _____

    combine with the _____ .

20. The spores of a fern are located on the _____ of

    the _____ .

Plants

True-False Assessment

Name: _____ **Date:** _____

Directions: Read each statement carefully. If the statement is true, put a **T** on the line provided. If the statement is false, put an **F** on the line provided.

_____ **1.** Plants make chemical energy by the process of photosynthesis.

_____ **2.** The leaves of plants absorb oxygen.

_____ **3.** Plants produce sugar.

_____ **4.** Oxygen is a by-product of photosynthesis.

_____ **5.** Chloroform is the substance that makes plants green.

_____ **6.** Plants use the energy from the wind to produce fuel.

_____ **7.** Nonvascular plants have stems.

_____ **8.** Liverworts distribute water and nutrients from cell to cell.

_____ **9.** Fibrous roots grow in one direction, straight down into the ground.

_____ **10.** Mosses are vascular plants.

_____ **11.** Petals protect seeds.

_____ **12.** Sepals are green leaves located beneath the flowers.

Plants

True-False Assessment *(cont.)*

_____ **13.** The stamen is the male part of the flower.

_____ **14.** Pollen is produced in the stamens.

_____ **15.** The plant's sperm cells are located on the anthers.

_____ **16.** Nonvascular plants have cones.

_____ **17.** Pollination occurs when seeds are dispersed.

_____ **18.** Nectar is a sweet liquid produced by flowers.

_____ **19.** Plant fertilization occurs when sperm cells combine with the egg.

_____ **20.** A spore is located on the pistil of a flower.

Plants

Matching Assessment

Name: _____   **Date:** _____

Directions: Read the items in both lists below and on page 63 carefully. Choose an item from List B that best matches an item from List A. Write the corresponding letter from List B on the line. You will have some left over.

List A	List B
_____ **1.** a process of making chemical energy	**A.** cones
_____ **2.** something leaves absorb	**B.** seeds
_____ **3.** plant fuel	**C.** veins
_____ **4.** photosynthesis by-product	**D.** cell to cell
_____ **5.** makes plants green	**E.** petals
_____ **6.** converted by plants into chemical energy	**F.** ferns
_____ **7.** vascular plant parts	**G.** anthers
_____ **8.** liverwort nutrient distribution	**H.** photosynthesis
_____ **9.** fibrous roots	**I.** chloroplasts
_____ **10.** hornworts	**J.** stamen to pistil
_____ **11.** seed protection	**K.** sugar
_____ **12.** sepal location	**L.** male plant parts

(GO)

Plants

Matching Assessment-Plants *(cont.)*

List A	List B
_____ **13.** pistil	**M.** sweet liquid
_____ **14.** stamens	**N.** oxygen
_____ **15.** sperm-cell location	**O.** carbon dioxide
_____ **16.** something conifers produce	**P.** sunlight
_____ **17.** pollination	**Q.** nonvascular
_____ **18.** nectar	**R.** chlorophyll
_____ **19.** combining of sperm cell and egg	**S.** stems, roots, leaves
_____ **20.** produces spores	**T.** fertilization
	U. grow in many directions
	V. female plant part
	W. beneath petals

Plants

Graphic Assessment

Name: _____   **Date:** _____

Directions: Look carefully at the diagram of the flower below. Locate and label the following flower parts: *petal, sepal, pistil, stamen, anther, leaves, stem.*

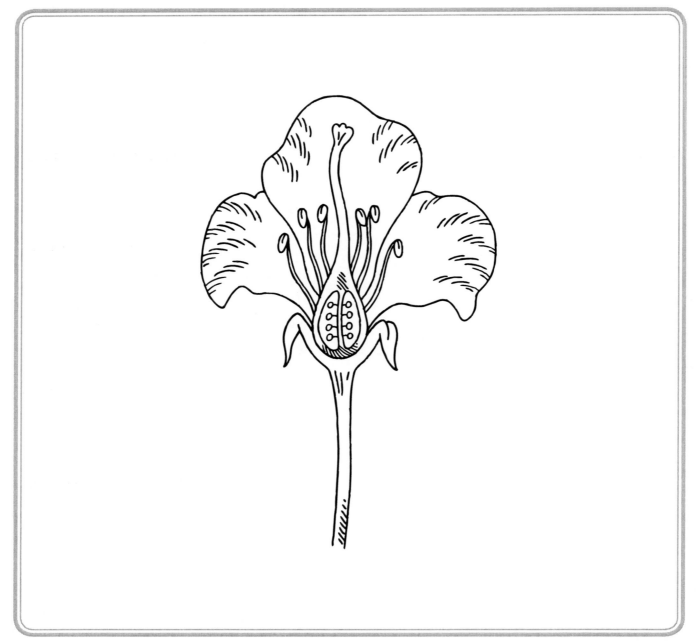

(GO)

Plants

Graphic Assessment *(cont.)*

Directions: The flowchart below shows the process that plants use to make seeds. Fill in as much detail as you can.

Pollination and Fertilization

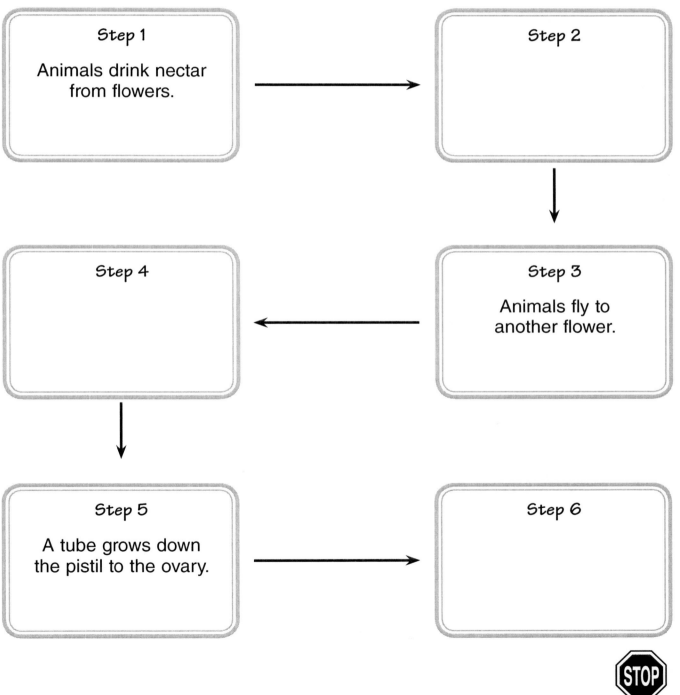

Step 1

Animals drink nectar from flowers.

Step 2

Step 4

Step 3

Animals fly to another flower.

Step 5

A tube grows down the pistil to the ovary.

Step 6

STOP

Ecosystems

Teacher Materials

 Teacher Preparation

Before you begin this unit, photocopy and distribute the following to students:

- Student Introductions (pages 69–71)
- Unit Vocabulary (pages 72–73)
- Student Briefs (pages 74–81)
- Assessments (pages 82–93)

 Key Unit Concepts

- Earth has five major land *ecosystems*.
- Everything in an ecosystem works together to keep it balanced.
- Animals have *niches*.
- *Producers* are organisms that make their own food.
- *Consumers* are organisms that eat other organisms.
- *Herbivores, carnivores, omnivores, scavengers,* and *decomposers* are definitions of organisms based on what they eat.
- Animals have adaptations that help them get and consume particular foods.
- *Food chains* and *webs* are relationships among organisms in ecosystems.
- Natural and man-made events change ecosystems.
- The actions of people often have very negative consequences on ecosystems.
- An *endangered* species is an animal or plant that is in danger of going extinct.
- An *extinct* animal or plant no longer exists on the planet.

 Discussion Topics

- Have students discuss the various ecosystems they may have visited. Ask them to describe the living and non-living parts of these ecosystems.
- Brainstorm a list of animals that have gone extinct.
- Have students discuss how they are adapted to live in their particular environment.

> See "Generic Strategies and Activities" on pages 8 and 9 for additional strategies useful to presenting this unit.

Ecosystems

Activities

 ### Brief #1: Types of Ecosystems

- **Make a Graph:** Ask students to research the top land speed of the following desert animals and create a graph that displays these speeds.

  black-tailed jackrabbit • caracal • roadrunner • rattlesnake • scorpion

- **Make a Mural:** Have students find out about six different animals that live in grasslands. Using a large piece of butcher paper, have students paint a mural that features these grassland animals.

- **Make a Diagram:** Have students research the different layers of a tropical rainforest: emergent layer, canopy, understory, forest floor. Ask them to make a diagram that shows some of the animals and plants at each level.

- **Write and Deliver a Narrative:** Ask students to select an animal from a specific ecosystem and research what its niche is. Then, ask students to write a short, first-person narrative from the point of view of that animal, explaining what its niche is and how it helps to keep the ecosystem in balance.

- **Make a Diorama:** Have students make a diorama that features an animal in its natural habitat.

- **Create and Maintain an Ecosystem:** Have students make and care for either an in-classroom aquarium or terrarium.

  Key Words: *roadrunner, rattlesnake, black-tailed jackrabbit, caracal, scorpion, grasslands ecosystem, layers of tropical rainforest, animals and niches, aquarium, terrarium*

 ### Brief #2: Food Webs and Food Chains

- **Make a Food Web or Food Chain:** Using index cards and paper clips, have students research and then make food chains. Each index card should have the name and illustration of an organism. Punch a hole in each card and then connect the chains with paper clips.

- **Play a Game:** Have students play a game in which they have to identify whether an animal is a carnivore, omnivore, or herbivore. Simply say the name of an animal. Ask students to respond by saying which type of eater the animal is.

- **Perform an Experiment:** Explain to students that mold is a decomposer because it breaks down an organism into smaller and smaller parts. Have students leave slices of bread overnight in the classroom. Add a teaspoon of water to the side of each slice of bread. Put the bread into a plastic baggie and seal the bag. Have students observe and record what happens to the bread over the course of a few days.

  Key Words: *food chains, carnivores, herbivores, omnivores, moldy-bread experiment*

Ecosystems

Activities *(cont.)*

 Brief #3: How Ecosystems Change

- **Create a T-Chart:** Have students create a T-chart that lists various events—both man-made and natural—that can cause change within an ecosystem.

- **Research and Report:** Ask students to conduct research to discover the status of seven animals. Have them complete the IUCN chart on page 69.

- **Make a Poster:** Have students make a poster that illustrates the ecosystem in which they live. Students should include as many living and non-living things that are a part of their ecosystem.

  Key Words: *ecosystems, IUCN*

 Activity Center

Animals and Ecosystems: Stock an activity center with books, magazines, and other resource material about various animals and the habitats in which they live. You may also want students to have access to a computer so that they can conduct Internet research. Instruct students to select one animal and research its habitat, what it eats, the larger ecosystem of which it is a part, and its status in the wild. Make several copies of the fact sheet that is on page 70. Make sure your center is also stocked with drawing materials.

 Internet Resources

- *http://www.mnh.si.edu/* — the official website of the Smithsonian National Museum of Natural History; includes photographs and lesson plans

- *http://www.mbgnet.net/* — the website of the Missouri Botanical Garden; contains a lot of information on ecosystems and biomes, including specific animals in each category

- *http://www.epa.gov/kids/* — the link to the EPA's Environmental Kids Club; includes games and activities

- *http://www.fws.gov/endangered/kids/index.html* — the U.S. Fish and Wildlife Service website

Ecosystems

Student Introduction: IUCN Chart

Name: _____   **Date:** _____

Directions: The International Union for Conservation of Nature and Natural Resources (IUCN) is an organization that keeps track of how populations of animals are doing on the planet. Use their website or other resources to complete the chart below.

IUCN website — *http://www.iucnredlist.org/*

Status	Animal
Least Concern	
Near Threatened	
Vulnerable	
Endangered	
Critically Endangered	
Extinct in Wild	
Extinct	

Ecosystems

Student Introduction: Activity-Center Fact Sheet

Name: _____ **Date:** _____

Directions: Fill out the facts below, then draw an illustration of your animal in the box.

— —

Name of Animal: _____

Habitat of Animal: _____

Animal's Ecosystem: _____

Animal's Food: _____

Status of Population: _____

Threats to Animal: _____

Ecosystems

Student Introduction: Ecosystems Word Web

Name: _____   **Date:** _____

Directions: Use this word web to help you brainstorm characteristics of ecosystems. What are some things that all ecosystems have in common? What are the names of some different ecosystems?

Ecosystems

Ecosystems

Vocabulary

1. **balance**—when all of the parts of an ecosystem are working as they should

2. **carnivore**—animal that hunts and eats other animals

3. **community**—all of the animals of different species that live in a particular ecosystem

4. **consumers**—organisms that eat other organisms

5. **decomposers**—organisms that feed off of dead plants and animals

6. **deforestation**—removing the trees from huge areas of land

7. **desert**—dry ecosystem that receives less than 10 inches of rain per year

8. **ecosystem**—all of the living and non-living things in a particular area

9. **endangered**—when the population of a plant or animal is so small it is in danger of going extinct

10. **extinct**—when there are no more of a species of a plant or animal on the planet

11. **food chain**—the path of the sun's energy as it passes from producers to consumers

12. **food web**—the relationship between all food chains within an ecosystem

13. **forest**—ecosystem with densely packed trees

14. **habitat**—the specific place in an ecosystem where an animal lives

15. **herbivores**—animals that eat only plants

Ecosystems

Vocabulary *(cont.)*

16. **landfill**—a huge hole dug into the ground into which trash is dumped

17. **niche**—the job of an animal in a particular ecosystem

18. **omnivore**—animal that eats both plants and other animals

19. **population**—the number of animals of the same species in a particular ecosystem

20. **predator**—a carnivore that hunts and kills prey for food

21. **producers**—organisms that do not consume other organisms

22. **rainforest**—wet ecosystem that receives a lot of sunshine and rain

23. **scavenger**—animal that eats only dead animals

24. **system**—something that is made up of different parts that work together

25. **tundra**—cold ecosystem where the ground is always frozen

Ecosystems

Brief #1: Types of Ecosystems

Focus

Earth has five major land ecosystems.*

The world in which we live is full of different kinds of systems. **A system is something that is made up of many different parts that all work together.** Systems can be natural or man-made. For example, the circulatory system is made up of the heart and blood vessels and other body parts that move blood and other substances through the body. The postal system is made up of mailboxes, stamps, letter carriers, and trucks that move mail from one place to another. In order for a system to operate well, all of the parts have to be working. If one part of a system breaks down, it has a big impact of the other parts of the system.

One of the natural systems on Earth is an ecosystem. **An ecosystem is all of the living and non-living things in a particular area.** For example, the plants, animals, rocks, soil, climate, water, and even people in a specific area are all part of an ecosystem.

Vocabulary

1. system
2. ecosystem
3. desert
4. rainforest
5. tundra
6. forest
7. grassland

 ### Types of Ecosystems

There are five major types of land ecosystems on Earth.* But in each large ecosystem there can be hundreds of smaller ecosystems. Even a puddle of water or a patch of grass can be considered a small ecosystem. The plants and animals present in a particular ecosystem are adapted to the conditions in that ecosystem.

* Note: The major types of ecosystems listed here are often referred to as *biomes*. The term *biome* is very closely related to the term *ecosystem*. Biomes are sometimes referred to as the largest of the *ecosystems*.

1. Desert

Deserts are one type of ecosystem. Deserts are very dry places. They receive less than 10 inches of rain per year. Deserts contain cactus, scrub grass, snakes, lizards, and meerkats.

2. Rainforest

In contrast to a desert, a rainforest can receive 70 inches of rain every year. There are thousands of species of plants and animals in a rainforest. Some parts of rainforests receive 12 hours of sunshine every day.

Ecosystems

Brief #1: Types of Ecosystems *(cont.)*

3. Tundra

The tundra is a cold area located either near the Arctic Circle or at high altitudes. The ground of the tundra is always frozen. Low grasses grow on the tundra. There are no trees. Mammals such as reindeer and mountain goats live in these areas.

4. Forest

In addition to rainforest, there are temperate forests and dry forests. Forests have lots of different types of plants and animals. Forests have many trees that grow very close to one another. In a forest, you may find squirrels, foxes, and raccoons.

> ## Vocabulary
> 8. population
> 9. community
> 10. habitat
> 11. niche

5. Grassland

Grasslands are large areas that are covered by grasses and low-growing plants. Unlike tundra, the ground beneath the grassland is not frozen. Many different types of animals, especially animals that graze, live in this type of ecosystem.

 ### Animals in Ecosystems

Different ecosystems are home to different types of animals. You would not expect to find a polar bear living in a rainforest or a lion living in the tundra! Each ecosystem has population of different animals. **A population is the number of animals of the same species living in one ecosystem.** For example, scientists think that the population of polar bears in the Arctic is about 30,000.

Each ecosystem is home to more than one species. You wouldn't expect to only find monkeys in a rainforest. **The grouping of all of the different species of animals in an ecosystem is called a community. The specific place in an ecosystem where an animal lives is called its habitat.** For example, a crocodile's habitat is in swamps in the rainforest.

> ### Fast Fact
> Bees pollinate Brussels sprouts, cucumbers, and strawberries.

Every animal, no matter how big or small or whether it lives in the desert or the rainforest, has a niche. An animal's niche is kind of like its job. **A niche is a certain role that an animal plays in helping to keep the ecosystem in balance and healthy.** For example, bees are called pollinators. Their niche is spreading pollen from flower to flower, which makes the reproduction of the flowers possible.

Ecosystems

Brief #2: Food Webs and Food Chains

Focus

All living things depend on energy from the sun for survival.

All of the living things in any ecosystem depend upon energy from the sun for their survival. Plants depend on the energy from the sun during photosynthesis to produce their own food. **In an ecosystem, plants are called producers because they produce their own food.**

But animals are not like plants. Animal can't produce their own food as plants do, so they survive by eating other living things. **Organisms that consume or eat other things are called consumers.**

Types of Consumers

There are three kinds of consumers in any ecosystem. They are herbivores, carnivores, and omnivores.

An herbivore is an animal that only consumes plants. Elephants, rabbits, and grasshoppers are some examples of herbivores. **A carnivore is an animal that only consumes other animals.** Lions, snakes, and wolves are carnivores. **An omnivore is an animal that eats both plants and animals.** People, bears, and pigs are omnivores.

There are some carnivores that are called scavengers. **A scavenger is an animal that only consumes dead plants or animals.** Vultures and hyenas are examples of scavengers. Other carnivores are predators. **A predator is a carnivore that hunts and kills prey.**

What an animal eats plays a part in how the animal looks. For example, carnivores have sharp teeth and claws. That's because they need to hunt other animals and tear raw meat apart. Herbivores have flatter teeth that are good for tearing and grinding plants.

Vocabulary

1. producers
2. consumers
3. herbivores
4. carnivore
5. omnivore
6. scavenger
7. predator
8. decomposers
9. food chain
10. food web

There is another important type of organism in any ecosystem. These organisms are called decomposers. **Decomposers are organisms that feed off of dead plants and animals.** Bacteria and fungi are important decomposers. Decomposers are not the same as scavengers. They actually can consume things that even scavengers leave behind. Decomposers feed off of leaves and other plants that fall to the forest floor, and they feed on the parts of dead animals that are left behind.

Ecosystems

Brief #2: Food Webs and Food Chains *(cont.)*

 Food Chain

Most all living things need energy from the sun to survive. **The path that the sun's energy takes as it passes from producers to consumers is called a food chain.** In a food chain, plants produce energy through photosynthesis, plants are consumed by herbivores, and herbivores are consumed by carnivores. Scavengers and decomposers consume anything that is left over.

The diagram below shows a food chain. Grass gets energy from the sun; gophers get energy from eating the grass; snakes get energy from eating the gophers; and hawks get energy from eating the snakes. The energy from the sun is being passed from one organism to another in the ecosystem.

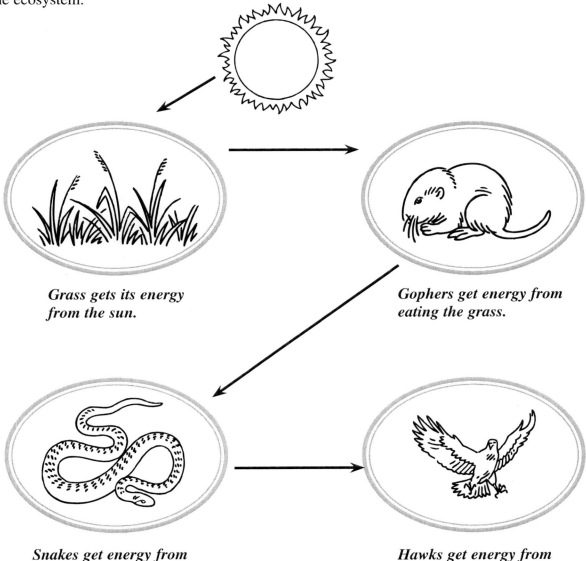

Grass gets its energy from the sun.

Gophers get energy from eating the grass.

Snakes get energy from eating gophers.

Hawks get energy from eating snakes.

Ecosystems

Brief #2: Food Webs and Food Chains *(cont.)*

 Food Web

Because there are many, many types of plants and animals in any one ecosystem, there are also many food chains. **A food web is the relationship between all of the different food chains in one particular ecosystem.** This illustration shows a food web. Remember that the arrows in a food web or chain point from the eaten to the eater.

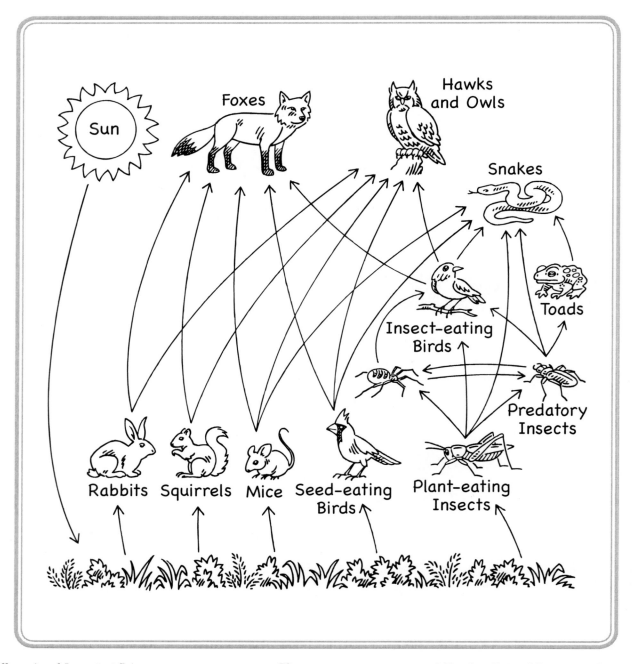

Ecosystems

Brief #3: How Ecosystems Change

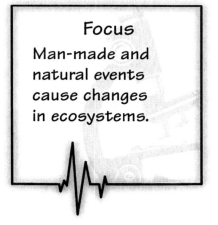

Focus
Man-made and natural events cause changes in ecosystems.

All ecosystems change. Sometimes they change because of natural events. A natural event is something that happens that is caused by natural forces. Blizzards, earthquakes, volcanoes, and tsunamis are all examples of natural events.

Sometimes they change because of a man-made event. A man-made event is an event that is caused by the actions of people. Pollution and deforestation are examples of man-made events.

Vocabulary

1. balance
2. landfill
3. deforestation
4. endangered
5. extinct

 Balance in Ecosystems

Everything in an ecosystem is in balance. **Balance means that all the living and non-living parts of the environment are working the way they are supposed to work.** Imagine your bicycle. It has pedals, wheels, brakes, and gears. When all of the different parts of your bike are working properly, it means that you can jump on it and ride safely!

But pretend that part of your bike is broken. Imagine that one of your tires needs air. You might still be able to ride your bike, but it definitely would not work as well as if both tires had all of the air they needed. Now imagine that instead of one tire being a little flat, you didn't have a tire at all! In that case, the bike would be broken. You would be unable to use it.

An ecosystem is kind of like your bike: when it is in balance, all of the different parts are working together. The plants and animals that live in that ecosystem can all get what they need to carry out their life processes. But if one part of the ecosystem is not working its best, or if a part of it is completely broken, the ecosystem stops working correctly. If an ecosystem stops working correctly, it puts all of the plants and animals that live in it at risk.

Ecosystems

Brief #3: How Ecosystems Change *(cont.)*

 ### The Role People Play

For thousands of years people have been using things in the environment to meet their basic needs. People use trees to make paper and houses. We use water to drink and to irrigate our crops. We use the land to grow food. People dig and drill fossil fuels like coal and oil out of the ground to use as fuel. But often the things that people do to the environment cause ecosystems to become unbalanced and to break.

 ### Water Pollution

Water in the form of rivers, streams, and lakes is a big part of most ecosystems. Many animals and plants depend on water for their survival. People, too, depend on water to live. All living things need water in order to survive. People often use toxic chemicals in farming and other industries. These hazardous materials wind up in water and cause a lot of damage to plants, animals, and people.

> ### Fast Fact
> Nearly 50% of all lakes and rivers in the United States are too polluted to swim in.

 ### Land Pollution

Did you ever wonder what happens to all of the trash that you put into trashcans at home or in school?   Most of this trash winds up in landfills. **A landfill is a huge hole dug in the ground into which trash is dumped.** The trash is buried in the hole and then covered up with dirt. Over time, the trash that is buried begins to decay and pollutes the land and soil.

> ### Fast Fact
> The average American throws away about 1,200 pounds of trash per year.

 ### Deforestation

Deforestation happens when huge areas of forest are cut down to make room for farms, houses, and/or roads. Trees are also cut down to use in the lumber industry. Each year thousands of acres of forest are destroyed.

Ecosystems

Brief #3: How Ecosystems Change *(cont.)*

 ## The Effect of Change

All of these things change ecosystems, and all of these changes impact plants, animals, and people. All of the animals that live in a particular ecosystem are specially adapted to live in that environment. They are not equipped to live anywhere else. Imagine a fish living on the land or a polar bear living in the desert. You would not expect these animals to survive.

Changes in ecosystems often bring about loss of habitat. When this happens, animals become endangered and can go extinct. **When an animal is endangered, it means that there is a good chance that the species will die out. When an animal is extinct, it means that there are no more of that species alive on the planet.** Once an animal becomes endangered or extinct, all of the other plants and animals in that ecosystem are affected. What might happen to plants if honeybees became endangered or went extinct?

Sometimes natural events can cause ecosystems to change and make plants and animals go extinct. Scientists think a huge natural event caused dinosaurs to go extinct millions of years ago. In recent years, the activities of people are usually the reason an animal has become endangered or extinct.

Recently Extinct Animals

Animal	Date of Extinction
Madeiran Large White Butterfly	2007
Black Rhinoceros	2006
Black-Faced Honeycreeper Bird	1974
Red Colobus Monkey	2000–2001
Golden Toad	1989

Earth is made up of many different types of ecosystems. If even one of those ecosystems breaks, it can have a big impact on the entire planet. For this reason, it's important for people to learn the ways in which their actions impact the environment.

 ## Protected Land

One way that people have learned to help the environment and ecosystems is to set aside land that is protected. If land is protected, that means that it either can't be used by people at all or it can only be used in a special way. Many of these areas in the United States are called national parks. Some important national parks in the United States are Yellowstone, Death Valley, and the Everglades. People in other countries in the world also set aside land that is protected.

By setting aside large areas, it means that we are protecting all of the plants and animals that live in those areas. This is important because all of the ecosystems on the planet are interconnected. Without healthy ecosystems, the planet could become a place that is difficult for people to live in.

Ecosystems

Multiple-Choice Assessment

Name: _____   **Date:** _____

Directions: Read each question carefully. Fill in the correct answer circle.

1. Which of the following is not an example of a system?

   Ⓐ postal system

   Ⓑ circulatory system

   Ⓒ car

   Ⓓ finger

2. What makes up an ecosystem?

   Ⓐ living things only

   Ⓑ non-living things only

   Ⓒ living and non-living things

   Ⓓ all plant and animal life

3. About how much rain does a desert receive in a year?

   Ⓐ more than 10 inches

   Ⓑ less than 10 inches

   Ⓒ exactly 10 inches

   Ⓓ none at all

4. Parts of which ecosystem receive 12 hours of sunshine every day?

   Ⓐ desert

   Ⓑ tundra

   Ⓒ grassland

   Ⓓ rainforest

5. In an ecosystem, what is meant by a population?

   Ⓐ the number of different species of animals

   Ⓑ the number of animals of the same species

   Ⓒ the number of plants and animals in an ecosystem

   Ⓓ none of these

Ecosystems

Multiple-Choice Assessment *(cont.)*

6. In an ecosystem, what is meant by a community?

Ⓐ the number of different animals in an ecosystem

Ⓑ the number of a single species in an ecosystem

Ⓒ the number of endangered animals in an ecosystem

Ⓓ all of the different animals in an ecosystem

7. Which of the following is an example of an animal's niche?

Ⓐ sleeping

Ⓑ reproducing

Ⓒ pollinating

Ⓓ all of these

8. Which of the following is a producer?

Ⓐ plants

Ⓑ animals

Ⓒ carnivores

Ⓓ omnivores

9. What does an herbivore eat?

Ⓐ animals

Ⓑ insects

Ⓒ dead animals

Ⓓ plants

10. The teeth of a carnivore are good for what?

Ⓐ tearing

Ⓑ grinding

Ⓒ softening

Ⓓ mashing

Ecosystems

Multiple-Choice Assessment *(cont.)*

11. What organisms eat what is not consumed by all other organisms?

    Ⓐ scavengers

    Ⓑ carnivores

    Ⓒ decomposers

    Ⓓ decompressers

---

12. What is the beginning of every food chain?

    Ⓐ plants

    Ⓑ the sun

    Ⓒ mammals

    Ⓓ decomposers

---

13. Which of the following statement best describes a food web?

    Ⓐ the relationship between all food chains in an ecosystem

    Ⓑ the path of the sun's energy from producers to consumers

    Ⓒ the interdependence of decomposers and scavengers

    Ⓓ the relationship between herbivores and carnivores

---

14. What can change an ecosystem?

    Ⓐ an earthquake

    Ⓑ a landfill

    Ⓒ a fire

    Ⓓ all of these

---

15. Why is pollution considered a man-made event?

    Ⓐ because it occurs naturally

    Ⓑ because it was created in a lab

    Ⓒ because pollution is created by people

    Ⓓ none of these

Ecosystems

Multiple-Choice Assessment *(cont.)*

16. If an ecosystem is in balance it means that

    Ⓐ all the parts are working as they should.

    Ⓑ one part of it is broken.

    Ⓒ the entire ecosystem is broken.

    Ⓓ there has been a natural disaster.

---

17. What is a landfill?

    Ⓐ a place where trash is buried

    Ⓑ a place where deforestation has occurred

    Ⓒ a place where coal mining has occurred

    Ⓓ none of these

---

18. What is deforestation?

    Ⓐ replanting a forest

    Ⓑ a fire in a forest

    Ⓒ an earthquake in a forest

    Ⓓ when a forest is cut down

---

19. If an animal is endangered it means that

    Ⓐ it is extinct.

    Ⓑ its population is healthy.

    Ⓒ the animal is probably a dangerous carnivore.

    Ⓓ it is in danger of going extinct.

---

20. If an animal is extinct it means that

    Ⓐ it no longer exists on the planet and never will.

    Ⓑ it is in danger of disappearing from the planet for good.

    Ⓒ it is a threatened species.

    Ⓓ it hasn't existed for over 100 years.

Ecosystems

Sentence-Completion Assessment

Name: _____ **Date:** _____

Directions: Read each statement. Fill in the word or words that best complete the sentence.

1. A _____ is something that is made up of different parts that

    work together.

2. An ecosystem is all of the _____ and _____ things in a

    particular area.

3. A desert ecosystem receives less than _____ inches of rain per year.

4. Parts of the _____ ecosystem can receive 70 inches of rain every year.

5. In an ecosystem, a _____ is the number of animals of the same species.

6. In an ecosystem, a _____ is all of the animals of different species.

7. An animal's _____ is kind of like their job.

8. Plants are called _____ because they make their own food.

9. An _____ is an animal that only eats plants.

10. The teeth of a carnivore are _____ because they are used for tearing meat.

GO

Ecosystems

Sentence-Completion Assessment *(cont.)*

11. Worms and fungi are examples of _____ .

12. The food chain begins with the energy from the _____ .

13. A _____ is the relationship between all of the food chains

    in an ecosystem.

14. An earthquake is an example of a _____ _____

    event.

15. An event caused by people is called _____-_____

16. If all of the parts of an ecosystem are working as they should, the ecosystem is said to be in

    _____ .

17. A _____ is a place where trash is buried.

18. _____ is when all of the trees in an area are removed.

19. An animal population that is low or in danger of dying out is called

    _____ .

20. A animal that no longer exists on the planet is said to be _____.

Ecosystems

True-False Assessment

Name: _____   **Date:** _____

Directions: Read each statement carefully. If the statement is true, put a **T** on the line provided. If the statement is false, put an **F** on the line provided.

_____   **1.** A bicycle is an example of a system.

_____   **2.** The living and non-living things in an area form a habitat.

_____   **3.** A desert receives over 10 inches of rain per year.

_____   **4.** Parts of a rainforest receive 12 hours of sunshine every day.

_____   **5.** A population of animals is all of the animals of the same species.

_____   **6.** A community is a group of scavengers.

_____   **7.** An animal's niche is like their job.

_____   **8.** An herbivore is an example of a producer.

_____   **9.** An herbivore only eats meat.

_____   **10.** Carnivores eat meat.

_____   **11.** Fungi is an example of a decomposer.

_____   **12.** The food chain always begins with the energy of plants.

Ecosystems

True-False Assessment *(cont.)*

_____ **13.** A food web is the relationship between all of the food chains in an ecosystem.

_____ **14.** An earthquake can't change an ecosystem.

_____ **15.** An event created by people is called man-made.

_____ **16.** An ecosystem in balance means that one or more parts of it are not working.

_____ **17.** A landfill is a deforested area.

_____ **18.** Deforestation means cutting down trees in a forest.

_____ **19.** An endangered animal is also called prey.

_____ **20.** An extinct animal no longer exists on the planet.

Ecosystems

Matching Assessment

Name: _____   **Date:** _____

Directions: Read the items in both lists below and on page 91 carefully. Choose an item from List B that best matches an item from List A. Write the corresponding letter from List B on the line. You will have some left over.

List A	List B
_____ 1. example of system	**A.** scavenger
_____ 2. parts of an ecosystem	**B.** earthquake
_____ 3. desert rainfall	**C.** carnivore
_____ 4. rainforest	**D.** small population
_____ 5. population	**E.** less than 10 inches
_____ 6. community	**F.** sun
_____ 7. niche	**G.** habitat
_____ 8. producer	**H.** balance
_____ 9. herbivore	**I.** living and non-living
_____ 10. sharp teeth	**J.** people
_____ 11. fungi	**K.** food web
_____ 12. beginning of food chain	**L.** animal job

GO

Ecosystems

Matching Assessment *(cont.)*

List A	List B
_____ **13.** food-chain relationship	**M.** plant-eating animal
_____ **14.** ecosystem change	**N.** place for trash
_____ **15.** cause of pollution	**O.** deforestation
_____ **16.** all parts working	**P.** 12 hours of sun
_____ **17.** landfill	**Q.** circulatory
_____ **18.** removal of trees	**R.** decomposer
_____ **19.** endangered animal	**S.** animals of same species
_____ **20.** extinct animal	**T.** no longer exists
	U. animals in an ecosystem
	V. plant
	W. tundra

STOP

Ecosystems

Graphic Assessment

Name: _____ **Date:** _____

Directions: In the space provided, draw an illustration of a simple food chain. Make sure to label all of the parts. The illustration has been started for you.

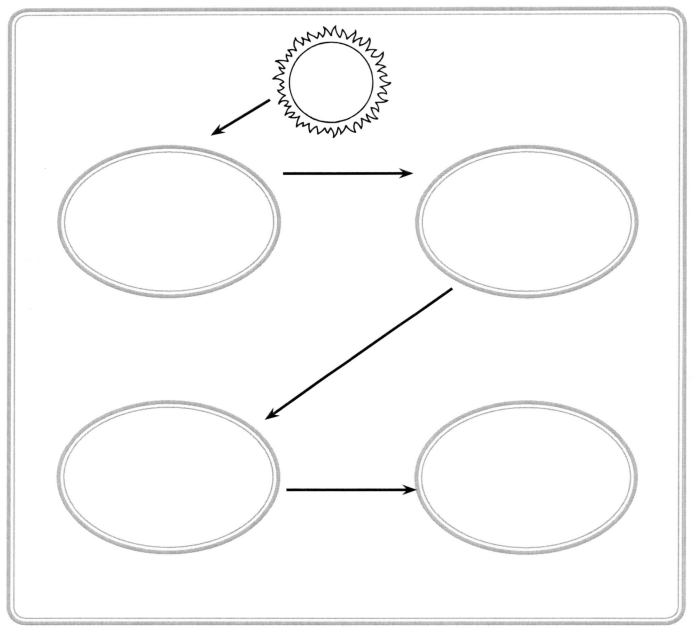

GO

Ecosystems

Graphic Assessment *(cont.)*

Directions: Look carefully at the ecosystems chart below. Fill in as much detail about each ecosystem as possible.

Types of Land Ecosystems	
Tundra	
Rainforest	
Forest	
Grassland	
Desert	

Water and Weather

Teacher Materials

 Teacher Preparation

Before you begin this unit, photocopy and distribute the following to students:

- Student Introduction (page 97)
- Unit Vocabulary (pages 98–99)
- Student Briefs (pages 100–106)
- Assessments (pages 107–117)

 Key Unit Concepts

- *Evaporation*, *condensation*, *precipitation*, and *accumulation* are the processes by which Earth's water supply is recycled.
- *Glaciers* contain most of Earth's freshwater.
- Three forms of matter occur naturally on Earth: *liquids*, *solids*, and *gases*.
- Water is a liquid form of matter, and it can be changed into a gas or a solid.
- Air is comprised mostly of nitrogen and oxygen.
- Changes in *air pressure* can create weather events.
- *Fronts* create weather.
- There are different types of clouds.
- *Meteorologists* use different tools to measure things like humidity, air pressure, temperature, wind speed, and wind direction.
- *Hurricanes* and *tornados* are powerful storms.
- Hurricanes are classified according to wind speed.

 Discussion Topics

- Why is it important for people to be able to accurately forecast the weather? How did people predict the weather in the past?
- What sorts of unusual or severe weather have you experienced?

> See "Generic Differentiated Strategies and Activities" on pages 8 and 9 for additional strategies useful to presenting this unit.

Water and Weather

Activities

 Brief #1: Earth's Water

- **Perform an Experiment:** Fill a third of a jar with water. Add ice and a few drops of food coloring. After about 15 minutes, observe the jar. What do you see on the inside and outside of the jar? What is causing these changes? (Condensation will appear.)

- **Perform a Play:** Have students write and perform a play that dramatizes the water cycle.

- **Have a Demonstration:** Boil a pot of ice cubes for the class so that they can see the ways in which temperature affects the state of water.

- **Write a Fictitious Conversation:** Ask students to write an imaginary conversation between different bodies of water. What might the conversation between the Indian Ocean, the Arctic Ocean, and a lake be like? What might they say to each other if they could talk?

- **Dramatize States of Matter:** Have students pretend that they are water in one of its three different states—a solid, a liquid, or a gas.

- **Make an Observation:** Place a bowl of water in the classroom. Have students observe what happens to the water over the course of 24 hours.

    Key Words: *water cycle, experiments*

Brief #2: Air, Wind, and Weather

- **Monitor the Weather Forecast:** Ask students to monitor the weather forecast for a period of seven days. Have them discuss how accurate the forecasts were.

- **Report the Weather:** Have students in your class provide a schoolwide weather report on a daily basis. Encourage students to use visual elements, like weather maps.

- **Create an Information Poster:** Have students create an informational poster that features various types of clouds. Make sure that they provide accurate illustrations and descriptions of the formations.

- **Meet a Meteorologist:** Invite a local meteorologist to your class to talk with students about their jobs.

- **Identify and Observe Clouds:** Take students outside a few times a week and have them observe and identify the types of clouds they see in the sky. Encourage them to make a connection between the cloud types and the current weather conditions.

    Key Words: *types of clouds*

Water and Weather

Activities *(cont.)*

 Brief #3: Hurricanes and Tornadoes

- **Research and Report:** Have students research the 10 largest hurricanes in recorded United States history. Have them report their findings, deciding for themselves what type of format to use.

- **Create a Tornado in a Bottle:** Take two empty 2-liter soda bottles. Fill one about three-fourths of the way full. Tape the two bottles together at the openings. Use packing tape or another type of strong tape. Turn the bottles so that the one containing the water is on the top. Turn that bottle in a clockwise circle so that you have all of the water spinning in the same direction. As the water empties from the top bottle into the bottom bottle, a vortex will form. Explain that this is what happens in tornado funnels.

- **Make a Chart:** Ask students to research the Fujita scale (tornado-intensity scale). Have them create a chart that shows how different-sized tornadoes are classified.

- **Make a Public-Safety Announcement:** Ask students to write and deliver a public-safety announcement about either hurricane or tornado preparedness. Ask students to record their announcements.

- **Provide Fast Facts:** Have students provide five additional fast facts about hurricanes or tornadoes. Make sure that the information provided is not already covered in the brief.

    Key Words: *largest hurricanes, Fujita scale, hurricane and tornado preparedness*

 Activity Center

Tracking and Graphing the Weather: Stock an activity center with graphing paper and colored pencils. Assign each pair of students two cities in the United States that have different climates. Using either the Internet or a newspaper, have students track the temperatures in their assigned cities for a one-week period of time. Ask them to create a double-line graph to display the data on their particular cities.

 Internet Resources

- *http://www.nhc.noaa.gov/* — the website for the National Hurricane Center; includes emergency preparation and up-to-the-minute tracking of tropical storms

- *http://www.nws.noaa.gov/* — the website for the National Weather Service; includes national, state, and county weather forecasts and warnings

- *http://www.fi.edu/learn/learners.php* — information for students from the website for the Franklin Institute

- *http://www.weatherwizkids.com/index.htm* — a site for kids designed by a meteorologist; includes games, experiments, and information about weather conditions

Water and Weather

Student Introduction: Weather Word Web

Name: _____   **Date:** _____

Directions: Use this word web to help you brainstorm characteristics of weather. What are some things that create different types of weather? What effect does weather have on the Earth's surface?

Weather

Water and Weather

Vocabulary

1. **accumulation**—the collection of water in the ground

2. **air**—the gaseous substance surrounding the Earth, composed mainly of nitrogen and oxygen

3. **air mass**—area of air with the same temperature and humidity

4. **air pressure**—the amount of force pushing on the atmosphere

5. **anemometer**—tool used to measure wind speed

6. **barometer**—tool used to measure air pressure

7. **cirrus**—clouds that are formed from ice crystals

8. **clouds**—condensed water vapor

9. **cold front**—when a cold-air mass bumps into warm air

10. **condensation**—the process that turns water vapor into clouds

11. **cumulonimbus**—large, heavy, dark storm clouds

12. **cumulus**—white, puffy clouds that usually mean dry weather

13. **evaporation**—the process of liquid water being turned into water vapor

14. **eye of the hurricane**—calm center of a hurricane

15. **front**—meeting place of two different air masses

16. **glacier**—slowly moving mass of frozen fresh water (ice)

Water and Weather

Vocabulary *(cont.)*

17. **humidity**—the amount of moisture in the air

18. **hurricane**—powerful storm with winds over 74 miles per hour

19. **hygrometer**—tool used to measure humidity

20. **ice**—frozen water; water as a solid

21. **meteorologist**—a person who studies and predicts the weather

22. **precipitation**—rain, snow, sleet, or hail that falls to the ground

23. **Saffir-Simpson Scale**—scale used to measure the strength of hurricanes

24. **storm surge**—a rise in sea level caused by a hurricane

25. **stratus**—low, grey clouds that usually mean rain

26. **thermometer**—tool used to measure air temperature

27. **tornado**—storm over land with a large funnel-shaped cloud

28. **tropical depression**—area of low pressure over the ocean where hurricanes are formed

29. **tropical storm**—thunderstorm with circular winds up to 74 miles per hour

30. **vortex**—area of spinning, whirling air and water inside of a storm

31. **warm front**—when a warm air mass meets a cold air mass

32. **water cycle**—the natural process that recycles the Earth's water

33. **water vapor**—condensed water; steam

34. **weather vane**—tool used to show wind direction

35. **wind**—force created when areas of low and high pressure meet

Water and Weather

Brief #1: Earth's Water

Focus

The water on Earth is recycled over and over again.

 Oceans

If you look at a photograph of our planet, Earth, from space, you will see large areas that appear blue. Most of that blue that you see is the Earth's massive oceans. We say that the Earth has five oceans—the Pacific, Atlantic, Arctic, Southern, and Indian—but really, they are just one huge ocean. Seventy-five percent of the water on Earth is in the ocean.

If you have ever gone for a dip in the ocean, you know that the water is very salty. Ocean water is way too salty for people to drink. If you drank ocean water, you would become ill.

The salt in the ocean is almost just like the salt that you use to put on food. It comes from rocks and soil. These things are washed away into the oceans when it rains.

Not all of the oceans in the world have the same amount of salt in them. For example, oceans that are located in warm, dry places—the Indian Ocean, for example—are much saltier than the oceans located in cool places—like the Arctic. That's because the warmer the water, the faster rocks and soil dissolve in the ocean and create salt.

 Freshwater

Most water that is in places other than the ocean is called freshwater. Freshwater is not salty like ocean water. The majority of Earth's freshwater is frozen in the glaciers. **A glacier is a huge piece of frozen fresh water.** The rest of Earth's fresh water is in rivers, lakes, and ponds.

 The States of "Water"

On our planet, matter can naturally occur in three different forms: liquid, solid, and gas (vapor). Water is a liquid, but it can be changed into a solid or a vapor. **Water that reaches zero degrees Celsius (or 32 degrees on the Fahrenheit scale) or below becomes a solid called ice.** Water that is between zero degrees Celsius (32 Fahrenheit) and 100 degrees Celsius (212° Fahrenheit) is a liquid called water. **Water that is above 100 degrees Celsius (212° Fahrenheit) becomes an invisible gas called water vapor.**

Vocabulary

1. glacier

2. ice

3. water vapor

4. water cycle

5. evaporation

6. condensation

7. precipitation

8. accumulation

Fast Fact

The Pacific Ocean is 165 million square kilometers.

Water and Weather

Brief #1: Earth's Water *(cont.)*

 The Water Cycle

All of the water that is on the Earth now is the only water that will ever be on the Earth. It is the same water that was here at the time of the dinosaurs! That's because the water on the planet is always being recycled through a process known as the water cycle. **The water cycle recycles the Earth's water supply from the ground to the atmosphere over and over again.** This process helps to clean the Earth's supply of water.

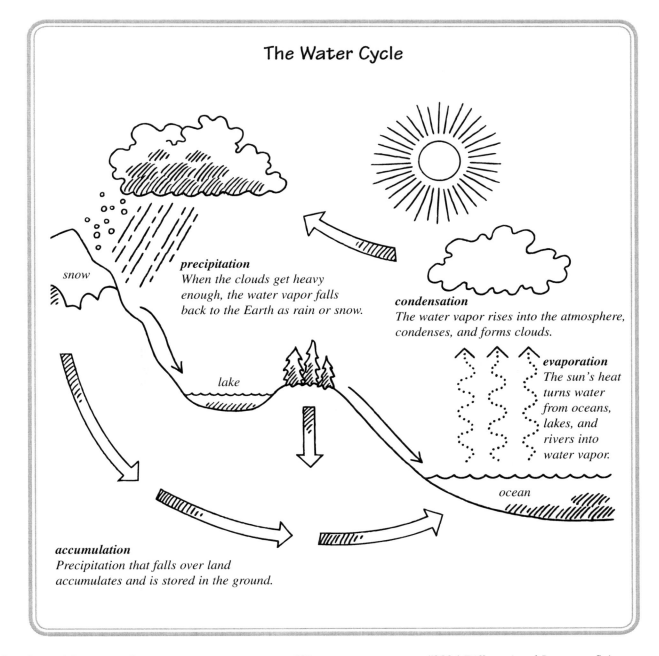

The Water Cycle

precipitation
When the clouds get heavy enough, the water vapor falls back to the Earth as rain or snow.

snow

condensation
The water vapor rises into the atmosphere, condenses, and forms clouds.

evaporation
The sun's heat turns water from oceans, lakes, and rivers into water vapor.

lake

ocean

accumulation
Precipitation that falls over land accumulates and is stored in the ground.

Water and Weather

Brief #2: Air, Wind, and Weather

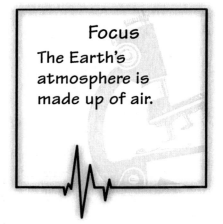

Focus

The Earth's atmosphere is made up of air.

The atmosphere of the Earth is an invisible gas called air. **Air is mostly a combination of two different gases: nitrogen and oxygen, with about 1% of it being made up of other gases, including carbon dioxide.** The most common gas in the atmosphere is nitrogen. The atmosphere of the Earth also contains water vapor. The Earth's gravity keeps this mass of air and water vapor around the planet like a blanket.

The atmosphere, or air, is made up of tiny particles. These particles have weight and take up space. There is space in between these particles. Because of this space, the particles have room to move closer together or farther apart. These tiny particles are what cause air pressure. **Air pressure is the amount of force created by the pushing of the gases in the atmosphere.** The more particles there are in an area, the heavier the air is; and the heavier the air is, the greater (or higher) the air pressure. The fewer the particles in a particular area, the lighter the air is. Lighter air means lower air pressure. Air pressure can push in all directions.

The temperature of the air is what causes changes in the tiny particles. When the air is warm the particles are packed very closely together. When the air is cool, the particles are not as densely packed.

If you have ever flown on an airplane or traveled to the top of a mountain you may have noticed that your ears pop. That's because you are going from an area of higher air pressure to an area of lower pressure. Your ears pop to keep the air pressure on the inside of you in balance with the air pressure on the outside of you!

Air particles are always on the move. **When an area of low pressure moves and meets an area of high pressure, wind is formed.** Air always moves from an area of high pressure to an area of low pressure.

Vocabulary

1. air
2. air pressure
3. wind
4. air mass
5. humidity
6. front

densely-packed air particles = higher air pressure

less air-particle density = lower air pressure

Water and Weather

Brief #2: Air, Wind, and Weather *(cont.)*

 ### Air Masses

The combination of air, water vapor, and temperature is responsible for creating weather. **An air mass is an area of air that has the same temperature and amount of water vapor. Humidity is the amount of water vapor that is in the air.**

Air masses are huge areas. Some are cold, while others are warm. Some air masses contain lots of water vapor, and others do not. When one type of air mass comes into contact with a different kind of air mass, rain, snow, thunder and lightening, and other types of weather are created.

The area where two different types of air masses meet or bump into each other is called a front. Cold air is much denser than warm air; and because it is denser, it moves more slowly than warm air. When a moving cold front meets a warm front, the denser cold air sinks beneath the warm air. This cools the warm air and pushes it up. As the air continues to cool and rise, it condenses into clouds. **A warm front is produced when a moving warm air mass bumps into a cold air mass.** A front is named according to which air mass is moving. **If the cold air mass is moving, it is called a cold front. If it is the warm air mass that is moving, it is called a warm front.**

Vocabulary

7. warm front

8. cold front

9. clouds

10. cirrus

11. stratus

12. cumulus

13. cumulonimbus

 ### Clouds

Clouds are formed through the process of evaporation. As the water on the surface of Earth is heated by the sun, it is turned into water vapor. **This water vapor rises up into the atmosphere and condenses to form clouds.**

When you look up into the sky, you may have noticed that there are many different types of clouds. Some are very white and puffy, and others can look heavy and dark. The way a cloud looks depends on what is going on in the atmosphere.

 ### Types of Clouds

✓ **Cirrus clouds** are the highest clouds in the sky. They look feathery and are made up of ice crystals. Cirrus clouds usually mean the weather will be dry and sunny.

✓ **Stratus clouds** are low, grey clouds that are close to the surface of the Earth. If you see stratus clouds, it means you might need an umbrella!

✓ **Cumulus clouds** are white and puffy. They look like floating cotton balls. These kinds of clouds usually mean dry weather.

✓ **Cumulonimbus clouds** are large, heavy, and dark. If you see these in the sky, it usually means a big storm is brewing!

Water and Weather

Brief #2: Air, Wind, and Weather *(cont.)*

 Tools Used with Weather

You know that different kinds of scientists use different types of tools to help them learn about the Earth. People who study the stars use telescopes, people who study diseases use microscopes, and people who study the weather use special tools, too. **A meteorologist is a person who studies and predicts the weather.** Here are some of the tools a meteorologist uses:

✓ **barometer:** a tool used to measure air pressure

✓ **anemometer:** a tool used to measure wind speed

✓ **thermometer:** a tool used to measure air temperature

✓ **hygrometer:** a tool used to measure the amount of humidity in the air

✓ **weather vane:** a tool used to measure the direction that the wind is blowing

Vocabulary

14. meteorologist

15. barometer

16. anemometer

17. thermometer

18. hygrometer

19. weather vane

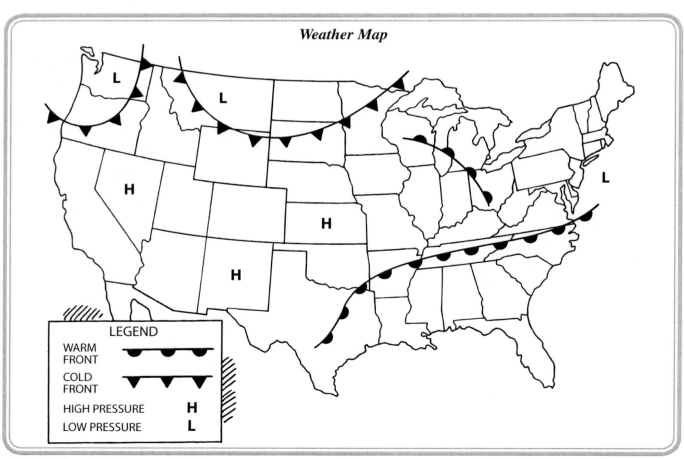

Weather Map

LEGEND

WARM FRONT

COLD FRONT

HIGH PRESSURE   **H**

LOW PRESSURE   **L**

Water and Weather

Brief #3: Hurricanes and Tornadoes

Focus

Hurricanes and tornadoes are some of the deadliest forces on the planet.

Hurricanes and tornadoes are weather events that can cause a lot of damage to people and places. They happen in particular places and under a specific set of conditions.

 Hurricanes

A hurricane is a powerful storm that has winds over 74 miles per hour that move in a circular direction.

Vocabulary

1. hurricane

2. tropical depression

3. tropical storm

4. eye of the hurricane

5. Saffir-Simpson scale

6. storm surge

Hurricanes begin as tropical depressions that form over warm oceans in areas of low air pressure. Because of this low pressure, winds blow in different directions and the water on the surface of the oceans is drawn upwards. This warm moisture then condenses into clouds.

When water turns into vapor, it recreates and releases a lot of heat. **The combination of low pressure, wind, and heat forms the tropical depression.**

As the heat increases and the winds become faster, the tropical depression becomes a tropical storm. As the air pressure continues to drop, thunderstorm clouds begin to move in a circular direction. When these circular winds reach 74 miles an hour, a hurricane is said to have formed.

The circular bands of storm clouds revolve around the eye of the hurricane. **The eye of the hurricane is the center of the storm.**
This area is calm and cloud-free.

The size and strength of a hurricane is measured on the Saffir-Simpson scale. The scale uses the speed of the wind to classify how powerful a hurricane is. Some hurricanes can be so powerful that they blow down buildings and destroy beaches.

The storm surge is a rise in sea level that is caused by the high winds of the hurricane.
The winds push huge waves onto the shore, which can cause major flooding. In some cases, the storm surge can cause the death of thousands of people.

Water and Weather

Brief #3: Hurricanes and Tornadoes *(cont.)*

 ### Hurricanes *(cont.)*

Because of how dangerous hurricanes can be, meteorologists use satellites and other special tools and instruments to try to predict when hurricanes will occur and to measure how big they will be. This makes it possible for people to prepare for the coming storm. Sometimes people can be evacuated from places that are in harm's way.

> **Fast Fact**
>
> All tropical storms are given the names of people.

Saffir-Simpson Scale

Category of Hurricane	Wind Speed
1	74–96 mph
2	97–110 mph
3	111–130 mph
4	131–155 mph
5	156 mph and up

 ### Tornadoes

Tornadoes are powerful weather events that happen over land. **A tornado is a storm that is characterized by a large, spinning, funnel-shaped cloud that touches the ground.**

Like hurricanes, tornados form in areas of low pressure. Tornadoes form inside of strong thunderstorm clouds. They can travel across land and can destroy everything that is in their paths. A tornado can have winds of over 300 mile per hour. **Inside of a tornado there is an area of spinning, whirling air and water called a vortex.**

Tornadoes usually happen in the spring and the summer. Tornado Alley is an area in the United States including Oklahoma, Nebraska, Kansas, and Texas where many tornadoes occur.

> **Vocabulary**
>
> 7. tornado
>
> 8. vortex

Water and Weather

Multiple-Choice Assessment

Name: _____   **Date:** _____

Directions: Read each question carefully. Fill in the correct answer circle.

1. How many named oceans does the Earth have?
   - Ⓐ 4
   - Ⓑ 1
   - Ⓒ 6
   - Ⓓ 5

2. Which of the following is not an ocean?
   - Ⓐ Atlantic
   - Ⓑ Pacific
   - Ⓒ Northern
   - Ⓓ Indian

3. Where does the salt in the ocean come from?
   - Ⓐ living organisms
   - Ⓑ rocks and soil
   - Ⓒ sand
   - Ⓓ condensed air

4. Which ocean would be the saltiest?
   - Ⓐ a northern ocean
   - Ⓑ a deep ocean
   - Ⓒ an ocean in a hot, dry place
   - Ⓓ a shallow ocean

5. Where is most of Earth's freshwater located?
   - Ⓐ glaciers
   - Ⓑ lakes, rivers, and ponds
   - Ⓒ under ground
   - Ⓓ in its core

Water and Weather

Multiple-Choice Assessment *(cont.)*

6. What is water that reaches zero degrees Celsius become?

Ⓒ ice

Ⓓ vapor

Ⓔ steam

Ⓕ liquid

---

7. If water is at a temperature of 72 degrees Fahrenheit, what state is it in?

Ⓒ solid

Ⓓ gas

Ⓔ vapor

Ⓕ liquid

---

8. If you want to change water into a gas, what to do you have to do?

Ⓒ make it colder

Ⓓ make it hotter

Ⓔ add salt to it

Ⓕ none of these

---

9. Which if the following best describes the water cycle?

Ⓒ condensation, motivation, accumulation, and evaporation

Ⓓ precipitation, evaporation, condensation, and accumulation

Ⓔ precipitation, salination, oxidation, and accumulation

Ⓕ precipitation, evaporation, irrigation, and accumulation

---

10. What might you need if there is a lot of precipitation?

Ⓒ mittens

Ⓓ a fan

Ⓔ an umbrella

Ⓕ a swim suit

Water and Weather

Multiple-Choice Assessment *(cont.)*

11. Where does accumulation happen?

    Ⓐ in the ground

    Ⓑ in the clouds

    Ⓒ in the leaves of plants

    Ⓓ none of these

---

12. Where is air pressure the highest?

    Ⓐ near the ocean

    Ⓑ top of a mountain

    Ⓒ in outer space

    Ⓓ all of these

---

13. When areas of low and high air pressure meet, what is formed?

    Ⓐ thunder

    Ⓑ rain

    Ⓒ wind

    Ⓓ earthquakes

---

14. What is humidity?

    Ⓐ the amount of particles in the air

    Ⓑ the amount of moisture in the air

    Ⓒ the amount of static electricity in the air

    Ⓓ a collection of cumulus clouds

---

15. When two air masses meet, it's called a

    Ⓐ back.

    Ⓑ collision.

    Ⓒ hurricane.

    Ⓓ front.

Water and Weather

Multiple-Choice Assessment *(cont.)*

16. Cirrus clouds are made up of what?

Ⓐ rain

Ⓑ ice crystals

Ⓒ snow

Ⓓ air particles

---

17. If you wanted to measure air pressure, you would use

Ⓐ a barometer.

Ⓑ an anemometer

Ⓒ a hydrometer

Ⓓ a weather vane.

---

18. All hurricanes begin as

Ⓐ tropical storms.

Ⓑ tropical clouds.

Ⓒ tropical depressions.

Ⓓ eyes.

---

19. All hurricanes have wind speeds over

Ⓐ 60 mph.

Ⓑ 74 mph.

Ⓒ 100 mph.

Ⓓ 50 mph.

---

20. What's a vortex?

Ⓐ a storm surge

Ⓑ the center of a storm

Ⓒ an area of spinning air and water

Ⓓ all of these

Water and Weather

Sentence-Completion Assessment

Name: _____ **Date:** _____

Directions: Read each statement. Fill in the word or words that best complete the sentence.

1. The number of named oceans on the Earth is _____ .

2. The Indian, Atlantic, Pacific, Southern, and _____

   are the Earth's oceans.

3. The salt in the ocean comes from _____ and _____.

4. The saltiest bodies of water in the world are located in places that are _____

   and _____.

5. The majority of the Earth's freshwater is located in _____ .

6. When water reaches zero degrees Celsius, it turns into _____.

7. Water that is 72 degrees is in a _____ state.

8. If you want to change water into a gas you have to make it _____.

9. Condensation, precipitation, _____ , and accumulation are part

   of the _____ .

(GO)

Water and Weather

Sentence-Completion Assessment *(cont.)*

10. Rain and snow are also called _____ .

11. Accumulation takes place in the _____ .

12. The amount of force pushing on things by the atmosphere is called _____ .

13. Wind is formed when areas of low and high _____ meet.

14. The amount of moisture in the air is called _____ .

15. When two air masses meet, it is called a _____ .

16. Ice crystals form inside of _____ clouds.

17. To measure air pressure, you would use a _____ .

18. Hurricanes begin as tropical _____ .

19. All hurricanes have wind speeds over _____ miles per hour.

20. An area of spinning air and water is called a _____ .

Water and Weather

True-False Assessment

Name: _____ **Date:** _____

Directions: Read each statement carefully. If the statement is true, put a **T** on the line provided. If the statement is false, put an **F** on the line provided.

_____ **1.** The Earth has five oceans.

_____ **2.** The Atlantic is not an ocean.

_____ **3.** The salt in oceans comes from rocks and soil.

_____ **4.** An ocean in a cold place would be saltier than an ocean in a hot place.

_____ **5.** Most of the Earth's freshwater is located in glaciers.

_____ **6.** When water reaches zero degrees Fahrenheit, it is turned into a liquid.

_____ **7.** Water that is 72 degrees Fahrenheit is a solid.

_____ **8.** To change ice from a solid to a gas you have to heat it up.

_____ **9.** Condensation is a part of the water cycle.

_____ **10.** Precipitation is another name for rain and snow.

_____ **11.** Accumulation takes place in clouds.

_____ **12.** Air pressure is highest at high elevations.

Water and Weather

True-False Assessment *(cont.)*

_____ **13.** When high and low air pressure meet, thunder is formed.

_____ **14.** Humidity is the amount of snow in the air.

_____ **15.** When two air masses meet, it's called a front.

_____ **16.** Cirrus clouds are formed from ice crystals.

_____ **17.** A hydrometer is used to measure air pressure.

_____ **18.** All tropical depressions begin as hurricanes.

_____ **19.** All hurricanes have wind speeds over 74 miles per hour.

_____ **20.** A vortex is a storm surge.

Water and Weather

Matching Assessment

Name: _____   **Date:** _____

Directions: Read the items in both lists below and on page 116 carefully. Choose an item from List B that best matches an item from List A. Write the corresponding letter from List B on the line. You will have some left over.

List A	List B
_____ 1. number of Earth's oceans	**A.** stratus
_____ 2. ocean salt	**B.** air pressure
_____ 3. location of freshwater	**C.** precipitation
_____ 4. when liquid water becomes solid	**D.** puffy
_____ 5. rain and snow	**E.** meeting of air masses
_____ 6. location of accumulation	**F.** hurricane scale
_____ 7. humidity	**G.** from rocks and soil
_____ 8. front	**H.** humidity-measuring tool
_____ 9. cirrus clouds	**I.** ice crystals
_____ 10. barometer	**J.** moisture in air
_____ 11. beginning of hurricane	**K.** anemometer
_____ 12. vortex	**L.** center of hurricane

GO

Water and Weather

Matching Assessment *(cont.)*

List A	List B
_____ **13.** funnel-shaped cloud	**M.** tropical depression
_____ **14.** condensation	**N.** weatherperson
_____ **15.** force of gases pushing in atmosphere	**O.** cloud formation
_____ **16.** cumulus clouds	**P.** tool to measure air pressure
_____ **17.** meteorologist	**Q.** in the ground
_____ **18.** hygrometer	**R.** glaciers
_____ **19.** eye	**S.** tornado
_____ **20.** Saffir-Simpson	**T.** swirling wind and water
	U. ice
	V. five

STOP

Water and Weather

Graphic Assessment

Name: _____ **Date:** _____

Directions: In the space provided, draw an illustration that shows how the water cycle works. Make sure to include labels with your illustration. Part of the illustration has been started for you.

Rocks and Minerals

Teacher Materials

 Teacher Preparation

Before you begin this unit, photocopy and distribute the following to students:

- Data Sheet (page 121)
- Student Introduction (page 122)
- Unit Vocabulary (pages 123–124)
- Student Briefs (pages 125–132)
- Assessments (pages 133–143)

 Key Unit Concepts

- *Minerals* are a non-living, natural part of the Earth.
- Minerals can be classified according to specific features.
- *Rocks* are made from minerals.
- *Sedimentary*, *igneous*, and *metamorphic* are the three types of rock.
- Rocks are recycled through the *rock cycle*.
- *Physical* and *chemical weathering* changes the surface of the Earth.
- *Erosion* changes the surface of the Earth.
- *Earthquakes* and *volcanoes* can rapidly change the surface of the Earth.
- *Gravity* is a force that contributes to how the surface of the Earth changes.

 Discussion Topics

- Have there been any recent natural events that have changed the surface of the Earth?
- What sorts of things in your local environment are made from rocks and minerals?

See "Generic Strategies and Activities" on pages 8 and 9 for additional strategies useful to presenting this unit.

Rocks and Minerals

Activities

 Brief #1: How Minerals Are Classified

- **Make a Birthstone Calendar:** Research what the birthstones are for each of the 12 months. For the upcoming year, make a calendar that features each month's birthstone. Include information about the birthstone, like its luster, hardness, and streak.

- **Make a Rock Collection:** Go on a rock-collecting expedition in your neighborhood. Gather at least 10 different-looking rocks to serve as the basis of a mineral collection. Display your rocks and include detailed information about them (e.g., shape, color, luster, hardness, size). Gather information regarding all student samples and create a class rock book.

- **Make a Poster:** Research crystal habits. Select three to four types of crystal and draw a poster that details how they are shaped. Make sure to include information about the particular crystal habits that you select.

  Key Words: *birthstones, types of crystals, crystal habits*

 Brief #2: Types of Rocks

- **Perform a Skit:** Research the rock cycle, then write and perform a skit that illustrates this natural process.

- **Create a Geologic Time Scale Newspaper:** Research the various geologic time periods (Precambrian, Paleozoic, etc.). Find out what plants and animals lived during these times. How did the surface of the Earth look then? What events caused it to change? After your research is complete, create a newspaper that includes feature stories, puzzles and games, obituaries, etc., regarding each time period.

  Key Words: *rock cycle, geologic time periods*

 Brief #3: How the Earth Changes

- **Perform an Experiment:** Fill a clear, plastic bottle full of water and then freeze it. Observe the bottle after it has been in the freezer for 24 hours. Record your observations. What has happened to the bottle? From this experiment, what conclusion can you draw about the process of physical weathering?

- **Perform an Experiment:** Place various materials in separate bowls: sand, wet soil, dry soil, and a piece of sod. Pour water over each material to demonstrate how water can change the land. Record your observations.

- **Make a Photo Album:** Make a book of photographs of places in the United States that are famous for how they have been eroded (e.g., Badlands National Park, Grand Canyon).

  Key Words: *Badlands National Park, Grand Canyon*

Rocks and Minerals

Activities *(cont.)*

 Brief #4: Earthquakes and Volcanoes

- **Make a Chart:** Make a chart that details the different classifications on the Richter scale.

- **Make a Public-Service Announcement:** Write and deliver an announcement about what to do in the event of an earthquake.

- **Perform an Experiment:** Using a slinky and a rope, demonstrate how seismic waves travel though Earth's crust.

- **Make a Graph:** Research the 10 most powerful earthquakes that have occurred in the country in which you live. Make a line graph that shows where they happened and what their magnitudes were.

- **Make a Flow Chart:** Make a flow chart that shows the stages of a volcanic eruption from magma chamber to lava flow.

- **Make a Map:** Most volcanoes occur along the Pacific Ring of Fire. Make a map that shows where the Ring of Fire is located and label the countries that are closest to it.

  Key Words: *Richter scale, earthquake safety, earthquake and volcano experiments, Pacific Ring of Fire*

 Activity Center

Mineral Hardness: In this activity, students will test the hardness of various minerals and record their findings on a data sheet. Stock your activity center with 10 different minerals (e.g., talc, gypsum, fluorite, quartz). Ideally, these minerals should be of varying levels of hardness. Have a series of different scratching instruments—penny, nail, metal nail file, plastic knife, etc. Include several copies of "Mineral Data Sheet" (page 121). Instruct students to scratch each mineral with each of the scratching instruments and then record their findings.

> ### Mohs Scale of Hardness
>
> 1. talc
> 2. gypsum
> 3. calcite
> 4. fluorite
> 5. apatite
> 6. feldspar
> 7. quartz
> 8. topaz
> 9. corundum
> 10. diamond

 Internet Resources

- *http://www.minsocam.org/MSA/K12/K_12.html* — a site from the Mineralogical Society of America that is designed especially for students

- *http://education.usgs.gov/* — the site for the United States Geological Survey; includes lesson plans

Rocks and Minerals

Mineral Data Sheet

Name: _____   **Date:** _____

Directions: Use this data sheet to record your findings.

Letter	Mineral	Can Be Scratched By
A		
B		
C		
D		
E		
F		
G		
H		
I		
J		

Rocks and Minerals

Student Introduction: Rocks and Minerals Word Web

Name: _____ **Date:** _____

Directions: Use this word web to help you brainstorm characteristics of rocks and minerals. What are rocks? How are they different from minerals? How are rocks made? What forces change them?

```
        ┌──────────────────────┐
        │                      │
        └──────────────────────┘

┌────────────┐          ┌────────────┐
│            │          │            │
└────────────┘          └────────────┘


┌────────────┐   ╭──────────────────╮   ┌────────────┐
│            │───│ Rocks and Minerals│───│            │
└────────────┘   ╰──────────────────╯   └────────────┘


┌────────────┐          ┌────────────┐
│            │          │            │
└────────────┘          └────────────┘

        ┌──────────────────────┐
        │                      │
        └──────────────────────┘
```

Rocks and Minerals

Vocabulary

1. **avalanche**—rapid movement of snow from a higher to a lower place

2. **chemical weathering**—changes to rocks caused by chemicals in the environment

3. **crust**—the outermost layer of the Earth

4. **deposition**—soil and rocks that are eroded from one place and taken to another

5. **earthquake**—shaking of the Earth caused by the movement of plates against the crust

6. **epicenter**—place on the Earth's crust above the focus of an earthquake

7. **erosion**—the movement of sediment from one place to another

8. **faults**—cracks in the Earth's crust

9. **focus**—place in the mantle where the earthquake begins

10. **hardness**—how easily a mineral can be scratched by another mineral

11. **igneous rocks**—rocks that are formed from magma

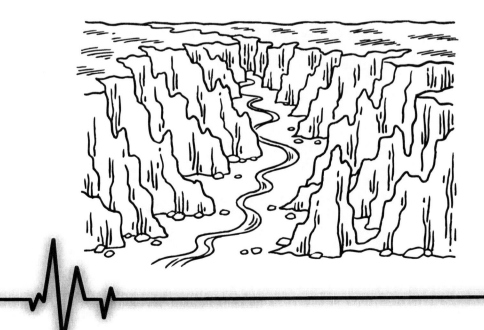

Rocks and Minerals

Vocabulary *(cont.)*

12. **lava**—molten rock which flows out of a volcano

13. **landforms**—natural features of the Earth's surface

14. **landslide**—rapid movement of land from a higher to a lower place

15. **luster**—how a mineral reflects light

16. **magma**—molten rock

17. **mantle**—portion of the Earth beneath the crust made up of plates

18. **metamorphic rocks**—rocks that have undergone a change

19. **minerals**—natural, non-living part of the Earth made from crystals

20. **Mohs scale**—chart that shows how hard different minerals are

21. **physical weathering**—changes to rocks caused by temperature, pressure, water, and ice

22. **plates**—huge pieces of mantle below the Earth's crust

23. **Richter scale**—scale that measures the strength of earthquakes

24. **rock cycle**—the constant process of rocks changing

25. **sediment**—eroded materials

26. **sedimentary rocks**—common rocks formed from bits and pieces of other things

27. **streak**—the color powder a mineral leaves behind after it has been scratched on a surface

28. **volcano**—the eruption of magma through a vent in the Earth

Rocks and Minerals

Brief #1: How Minerals Are Classified

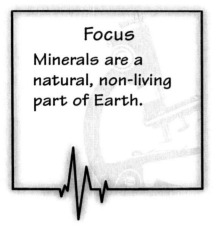

Focus
Minerals are a natural, non-living part of Earth.

You know that scientists classify many different things to make them easier to study and understand. Scientists classify plants, animals, and different types of climate. Scientists also classify minerals. **Minerals are a natural, non-living part of Earth. Minerals are what rocks are made out of.**

The Earth is full of different kinds of minerals. Each type of mineral is made up of crystals that are different shapes. For example, the crystals in the mineral pyrite are cube-shaped, and the crystals in the mineral hematite are shaped like hexagons. There are about 3,000 minerals on Earth. Most rocks are made up of at least two different kinds of mineral.

 ### Characteristics of Minerals

There are many ways by which to tell one mineral from another. One of the features that scientists look at is called *luster*. **Luster means how the mineral reflects light.** The luster of a mineral can be described in such ways as waxy, silky, or dull. The luster of the minerals gold and silver is called metallic.

Another way in which minerals are classified is by their hardness. *Hardness* **means how easily a mineral can be scratched by another mineral.** For example, talc is a mineral that is very soft. If you scratched it with the tip of a pen, it would crumble. Diamond is the hardest mineral. A diamond can cut through any other mineral.

Vocabulary
1. minerals
2. luster
3. hardness
4. Mohs scale
5. streak

The Mohs scale of mineral hardness is a chart that shows how hard different minerals are. It ranks minerals on a scale from 1–10—one is the softest mineral; ten is the hardest.

Fast Fact
The typical shape and size in which a mineral's crystals grow is called its "habit."

Streak is a third way in which minerals can be classified. **Streak is the color of the powder the mineral leaves behind when it is scratched in a surface.** For example, fluorite leaves a white streak, and galena leaves a grey streak.

There are also other features of minerals—including color, transparency, and crystal form—that scientists look at when they are classifying minerals.

Rocks and Minerals

Brief #1: How Minerals Are Classified *(cont.)*

Properties of Minerals

Mineral	Luster	Hardness	Streak
Graphite	metallic, earthy	1–2	black
Pyrite	glistening, metallic	6–6.8	greenish black
Rose Quartz	glassy	7	white
Topaz	glassy	8	white
Hematite	metallic	5.5–6.5	red
Gypsum	silky, pearly	1.5–2	white
Sphalerite	brilliant, diamond-like	3.4–4	yellow or light brown

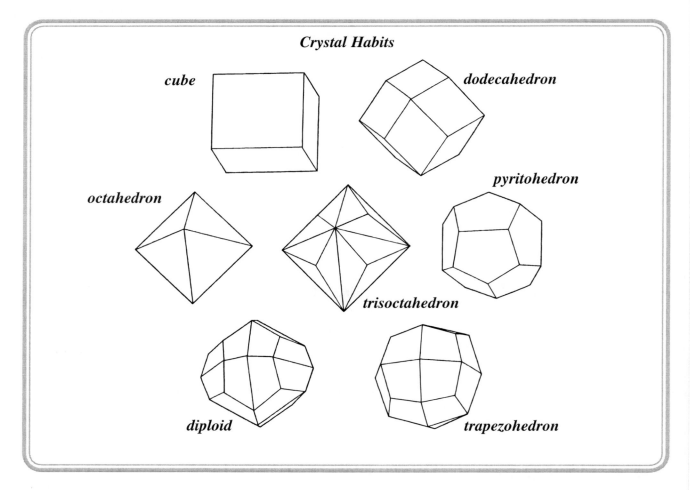

Crystal Habits

cube   dodecahedron   pyritohedron   octahedron   trisoctahedron   diploid   trapezohedron

Rocks and Minerals

Brief #2: Types of Rocks

> ### Focus
> There are three basic types of rock on Earth.

Rocks are a natural, non-living part of the Earth. They are made up of minerals. Most rocks have two or more minerals in them. There are three basic types of rocks on planet Earth.

 Sedimentary Rocks

Sedimentary rocks are the most common type of rock on Earth. They are formed from dead plants, animals, soil, shells, and bits of other rocks.

Wind, rain, and other types of weather move this material from one place to another. This process is called erosion. This eroded material winds up in lakes, rivers, and on the land. **The eroded material is called sediment.**

As time passes, more and more sediment is created, and it is deposited in layers. These layers of sediment weigh and press down on one another. Clay that is in the ground begins to fill in among the sediment. The clay and sediment harden and form rocks.

Because sedimentary rocks are made from bits and pieces of a lot of different material, there can be different types of sedimentary rock.

- ✓ **Limestone** is created from the skeletons and shells of animals that lived in the past. Chalk is one type of limestone.
- ✓ **Sandstone** is made from grain-sized pieces of quartz.
- ✓ **Conglomerate** is made from individual stones.

 Igneous Rocks

Igneous rocks are formed from magma. Below the crust of the Earth there is rock that is so hot it is partially in a liquid state. **This molten rock is called magma.**

The surface of the Earth is full of cracks. Most of the molten rock rises to the surface of the Earth and flows out through these cracks. When this magma cools, it forms igneous rocks. Magma also erupts out of volcanoes as lava. When lava cools, it also forms igneous rock. Just as there are different types of sedimentary rock, there are different types of igneous rock. All igneous rocks are formed from magma, but one of the things that makes them different from each other is how quickly the magma cools.

- ✓ **Basalt** is a type of igneous rock that cooled very quickly. Most of the floor of the ocean is made of basalt.
- ✓ **Obsidian** is also an igneous rock that has cooled quickly. Obsidian was used by prehistoric people to make tools.
- ✓ **Granite** is a type of igneous rock that cools slowly. Granite is often used in building.

Rocks and Minerals

Brief #2: Types of Rocks *(cont.)*

 Metamorphic Rocks

Metamorphic rocks begin as sedimentary or igneous rocks. **Metamorphic rocks are rocks that have undergone a change.** Heat and pressure are forces that are at work beneath the crust of the Earth. As igneous and sedimentary rocks are heated and squeezed, they can change their forms. Sometimes heat and pressure actually cause the tiny crystals that make up sedimentary or igneous rocks to change shape and size. At other times, these forces can cause new and different minerals to form altogether.

> **Vocabulary**
> 1. sedimentary rock
> 2. sediment
> 3. igneous rocks
> 4. magma
> 5. metamorphic rocks
> 6. rock cycle

✓ **Marble** is a metamorphic rock. It is made from limestone that has been heated and pressurized. The heat and pressure on the limestone actually changes its crystal habit—and, as a result, changes the limestone into marble.

✓ **Slate** is another type of metamorphic rock. It is often used to make blackboards. Slate is formed from the sedimentary rock shale. Heat and pressure cause the minerals in the shale to form rows. For this reason, it is very easy to split slate apart into layers.

 The Rock Cycle

Rocks are constantly undergoing changes. The process of erosion, heat, pressure, and natural events (like volcanoes) cause rocks to change from one type to another. **This constant process of rocks changing form is called the rock cycle.** Rocks, like water, are always being recycled, but it takes a very long time for one rock to become another type of rock. Scientists divide the history of Earth into periods. The oldest rocks on Earth are from the Precambrian period, the youngest from the Cenozoic period.

Geologic Time Scale

Precambrian Era	Paleozoic Era	Mesozoic Era	Cenozoic Era
4 billion to 542 million years ago	542 to 251 million years ago	251 to 65.5 million years ago	65.5 million years ago to present

Rocks and Minerals

Brief #3: How the Earth Changes

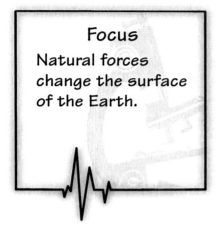

Focus
Natural forces change the surface of the Earth.

The outer layer of the Earth is called the crust. The crust of the Earth is made up of rocks and other loose materials. The Earth's crust is between 6 and 25 miles thick, and it covers the entire surface of the planet.

The surface of the Earth is covered with landforms. **Landforms are natural features of the Earth, like mountains, rivers, and coastlines.** The way the land looks on Earth is a result of many different natural processes that are always at work changing it. The Earth today looks very different from the Earth that existed in the past; and the Earth of the future will look different from the way it looks now.

 Weathering

One of the processes that changes the land is called weathering. **During physical weathering, temperature, water, ice, melting snow, and pressure change the size of rocks.** Large rocks can be broken down into smaller rocks.

Imagine rocks that are scattered all over the ground in a desert. The heat of the day causes the rocks to expand (get bigger). But at night, when the sun sets and the temperature drops, the rocks cool off and contract (get smaller). During this time, they can split and crack.

Freezing temperatures can also make rocks break. In very cold places, water can seep into the cracks of rocks. As the water freezes and turns into ice, it expands. The expansion of the ice in the cracks and crevices of the rocks can cause them to crack and break apart.

Vocabulary

1. crust
2. landforms
3. physical weathering
4. chemical weathering
5. erosion

Plants can also cause rocks to change. Both small and large plants can grow between the cracks in rocks. As the roots get larger and larger, they can cause the rocks to crack. Have you ever noticed what happens to the sidewalk when the roots of a big tree grow beneath it? This is an example of how plants can cause rocks to change.

Chemical weathering is another way in which rocks change. **During chemical weathering, water and chemicals in the environment seep into rocks and actually change what the rocks are made of.** This causes the rocks to break down. For example, Earth's atmosphere is full of carbon dioxide. Carbon dioxide is a by-product of photosynthesis. Carbon dioxide can mix with water to form a kind of acid that covers the surface of rocks and wears them away until they break into smaller and smaller pieces. Think of all of the chemicals that people put in the environment, like exhaust from cars and pesticides that are used in farming. All of these chemicals can cause rocks to wear away and break up into smaller pieces.

Rocks and Minerals

Brief #3: How the Earth Changes *(cont.)*

 ## Erosion

Erosion is another process that changes the way that the Earth looks. Erosion is different from physical and chemical weathering. During weathering, the rocks that are changed stay in one place. **During erosion, rocks and soil are moved from one place to another.** Things like hurricanes, wind, and melting ice can cause huge amounts of erosion. The Great Lakes were formed by huge glaciers that moved over the land and carved massive holes. Those holes eventually filled with water.

If you stand at the ocean's edge on a beach, you will see erosion in action. As waves push and pull on the sand of the shore, it moves out from underneath of your feet. But where does the sand that is eroded from beneath your feet go? **Soil and rocks that are eroded are taken from one place and carried or deposited. This process is called deposition.** During deposition, eroded material or sediment is set down in layers.

> ## Vocabulary
>
> 6. deposition
>
> 7. landslide
>
> 8. avalanche

 ## Rapid Change

Physical and chemical weathering and erosion are processes that usually occur over long periods of time. There are some other natural forces on the Earth that can cause changes to the land instantly.

Gravity is a natural force that is constantly pulling down on everything contained on the Earth. Gravity pulls things from high places to low places. You know that if you release a pencil from your hand that there is only one direction in which it will go. This same force pulls on mountains, rivers, and rocks.

During a big storm, water seeps into the ground and loosens it up. Then the force of gravity can pull the loosened ground down quickly. **The rapid movement of land from a high place to a lower place is called a landslide.** A similar

thing can happen in colder places where there are huge amounts of snow high up on mountains. **The weight of the snow, along with the force of gravity, pulls the snow quickly down the mountain. This event is called an avalanche.** Both avalanches and landslides are examples of how natural forces can change the surface of the Earth.

Rocks and Minerals

Brief #4: Earthquakes and Volcanoes

> ### Focus
> Earthquakes and volcanoes can rapidly change the surface of the Earth.

The crust of the Earth is on top of something called the mantle. **The mantle of the Earth is not one solid piece; it consists of several large pieces called plates.** Think of the mantle as huge pieces of a massive jigsaw puzzle. These plates are constantly in motion. They are moving beneath the Earth's crust.

 ### Earthquakes

The Earth's crust contains many cracks. These cracks are called faults. Sometimes the Earth's crust releases energy, and this energy can cause the crust to get stuck. Even though the crust is stuck, the plates on the mantle continue to move. **The moving plates beneath the stuck crust shake and vibrate. This is called an earthquake.**

The place beneath the crust, in the mantle where the earthquake begins, is called the focus. The epicenter of an earthquake is located on the crust. It is the place directly above the focus.

Earthquakes can be large or small. Large (and even medium-sized) earthquakes can change the surface of the Earth within a matter of seconds. Large holes can open up in the Earth, and huge pieces of rock can be pushed out onto the surface. When earthquakes happen in places where people live, they can destroy fuel and electricity lines. Fires can occur.

Earthquakes are measured on the Richter scale. This scale classifies earthquakes according to their magnitude from 1 to 10. One is the smallest earthquake, and 10 the largest. The largest earthquake ever recorded happened in the country of Chile in 1960. It measured 9.5 on the Richter scale.

> ### Vocabulary
> 1. mantle
> 2. plates
> 3. faults
> 4. earthquakes
> 5. focus
> 6. epicenter
> 7. Richter scale
> 8. volcano
> 9. lava

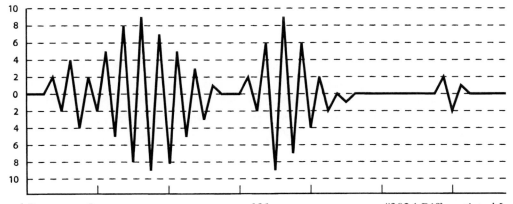

Rocks and Minerals

Brief #4: Earthquakes and Volcanoes *(cont.)*

 ### Volcanoes

Deep inside of the Earth's mantle is rock that is so hot it is partly liquefied. This magma also contains a lot of gas. The Earth's crust contains many openings. These openings are called vents. **Sometimes the magma deep in the Earth's mantle boils and erupts out of one of these vents. This event is called a volcano.** Molten rock, gas, and ash spew out of the vent. **The molten rock that flows from a volcano is called lava.**

Shield, composite, and cinder cone are types of volcanoes. Volcanoes can also be active, dormant, or extinct. An active volcano is a volcano that erupts on a pretty regular basis. Mount Loa and Mount Kilauea are two active volcanoes located in the state of Hawaii.   If we count the part of it that is beneath the ocean's surface, Mount Loa is taller than Mount Everest. It has erupted 15 times since 1900.

A dormant volcano is a volcano that hasn't erupted for a very long time. Mount Pierce, located in British Columbia, has not erupted for 9,000 years. An extinct volcano is a volcano that has not erupted since the beginning of recorded history and is very unlikely to ever erupt again. The Yellowstone Caldera, located in Yellowstone National Park, has not erupted for over 600,000 years.

Like earthquakes, volcanoes can change the Earth dramatically in a matter of minutes. A lava flow can destroy everything in its path, including forests and towns. Once the lava cools, new rock begins to form.

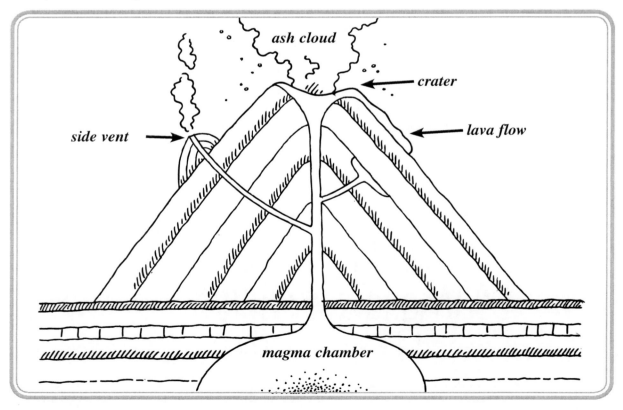

Rocks and Minerals

Multiple-Choice Assessment

Name: _____ **Date:** _____

Directions: Read each question carefully. Fill in the correct answer circle.

1. What are minerals made from?

    Ⓐ rocks

    Ⓑ quartz

    Ⓒ crystals

    Ⓓ luster

2. How are minerals different than rocks?

    Ⓐ rocks are harder

    Ⓑ minerals are brighter

    Ⓒ minerals are what rocks are made from

    Ⓓ rocks are what minerals are made from

3. What is a mineral's luster?

    Ⓐ how the mineral reflects light

    Ⓑ how hard the mineral is

    Ⓒ what color the mineral is

    Ⓓ the crystal habit

4. If a mineral ranks 7 on the Mohs scale, it means that it is

    Ⓐ pretty soft.

    Ⓑ liquid.

    Ⓒ pretty hard.

    Ⓓ none of these

5. A mineral's streak is

    Ⓐ how it smells.

    Ⓑ how shiny it is.

    Ⓒ how dense it is.

    Ⓓ the color powder it leaves behind after being scratched.

Rocks and Minerals

Multiple-Choice Assessment *(cont.)*

6. What type of rock is formed from bits and pieces of other materials?

   Ⓐ metamorphic

   Ⓑ sedimentary

   Ⓒ igneous

   Ⓓ none of these

---

7. What is limestone made from?

   Ⓐ the shells and skeletons of dead animals

   Ⓑ the fossils of leaves

   Ⓒ lava

   Ⓓ mammal bones

---

8. In a piece of conglomerate rock, you would see

   Ⓐ individual stones.

   Ⓑ fossils.

   Ⓒ quartz.

   Ⓓ magma

---

9. Magma forms

   Ⓐ sedimentary rocks.

   Ⓑ metamorphic rocks.

   Ⓒ sandstone.

   Ⓓ igneous rocks.

---

10. Basalt

   Ⓐ cools quickly.

   Ⓑ cools slowly.

   Ⓒ is very soft.

   Ⓓ all of these

Rocks and Minerals

Multiple-Choice Assessment *(cont.)*

11. Which of the following was used to make tools?

    Ⓐ talc

    Ⓑ conglomerate

    Ⓒ obsidian

    Ⓓ none of these

12. Metamorphic rocks are rocks that have

    Ⓐ changed.

    Ⓑ exploded.

    Ⓒ melted.

    Ⓓ cracked.

13. In which geologic period would you find the youngest rocks?

    Ⓐ Precambrian Era

    Ⓑ Cenozoic Era

    Ⓒ Paleozoic Era

    Ⓓ Mesozoic Era

14. About how thick is the Earth's crust?

    Ⓐ 100 feet

    Ⓑ 8,000–20,000 kilometers

    Ⓒ 6–25 miles

    Ⓓ 1 mile

15. How is erosion different from physical weathering?

    Ⓐ During erosion things are moved from one place to another.

    Ⓑ During erosion things stay in one place.

    Ⓒ During physical weathering rocks undergo a chemical change.

    Ⓓ During physical weathering rocks are smashed.

Rocks and Minerals

Multiple-Choice Assessment *(cont.)*

16. A rise in temperature causes rocks to

Ⓐ contract.

Ⓑ melt.

Ⓒ expand.

Ⓓ move.

---

17. What is the main force that causes landsides?

Ⓐ friction

Ⓑ gravity

Ⓒ magnetism

Ⓓ chemical change

---

18. What is the upper mantle of the Earth made of?

Ⓐ large pieces of rock called plates

Ⓑ magma

Ⓒ lava

Ⓓ faults

---

19. What's an epicenter?

Ⓐ the place on the crust above the magma

Ⓑ the place in the mantle where an earthquake begins

Ⓒ a vent

Ⓓ the place on the crust above the focus

---

20. Earthquakes and volcanoes can

Ⓐ make slow changes to the Earth.

Ⓑ make rapid changes to the Earth.

Ⓒ slow the force of gravity.

Ⓓ create dormant volcanoes.

Rocks and Minerals

Sentence Completion Assessment

Name: _____ **Date:** _____

Directions: Read each statement. Fill in the word or words that best complete the sentence.

1. Minerals are made from _____ .

2. Minerals form _____ .

3. How a mineral reflects light is called its _____ .

4. A mineral that ranks 10 on the Mohs scale means that it is very _____ .

5. The color powder a mineral leaves behind after it's been scratched is called its

   _____ .

6. _____ rock is formed from the bits and

   pieces of other materials.

7. The shells and skeletons of dead animals make up _____ .

8. Individual stones would be visible in _____ .

9. Magma forms _____ rocks.

Rocks and Minerals

Sentence Completion Assessment *(cont.)*

10. Basalt cools _____ .

11. Obsidian was used by people to make _____ .

12. _____ rocks are rocks that began as another type of rock and

    have since changed.

13. During the Cenozoic Era you would find the _____ rocks.

14. The Earth's crust is between _____ and _____ miles thick.

15. During erosion material is _____ from one place to another.

16. A rise in temperature can cause rock to _____ .

17. Gravity contributes to avalanches and _____ .

18. The large pieces of rock that form the mantle are called _____ .

19. The location on the Earth's crust directly above the focus of an earthquake is called the

    _____ .

20. An opening in the Earth's crust is called a _____ .

STOP

Rocks and Minerals

True-False Assessment

Name: _____ **Date:** _____

Directions: Read each statement carefully. If the statement is true, put a **T** on the line provided. If the statement is false, put an **F** on the line provided.

_____ **1.** Minerals are made from crystals.

_____ **2.** Minerals are made from rocks.

_____ **3.** A mineral's luster is how hard it is.

_____ **4.** The Mohs scale ranks the hardness of minerals.

_____ **5.** The streak of a mineral is how well it reflects light.

_____ **6.** Sedimentary rocks are formed from bits and pieces of other material.

_____ **7.** Limestone is made from skeletons and shells.

_____ **8.** In a piece of conglomerate, you would expect to see a fossil.

_____ **9.** Magma forms igneous rocks.

_____ **10.** Basalt cools slowly.

_____ **11.** Talc was used to make tools.

_____ **12.** Metamorphic rocks are rocks that have undergone a change.

Rocks and Minerals

True-False Assessment *(cont.)*

_____ **13.** The youngest rocks were formed during the Paleozoic Era.

_____ **14.** The Earth's crust is about 2 miles thick.

_____ **15.** During physical weathering, temperature can cause changes to rocks.

_____ **16.** When rocks get very hot, they contract.

_____ **17.** A landslide is partly caused by gravity.

_____ **18.** The Earth's crust is made up of large plates.

_____ **19.** An epicenter is the location of the focus of an earthquake.

_____ **20.** Earthquakes and volcanoes can rapidly change the surface of the Earth.

Rocks and Minerals

Matching Assessment

Name: _____   **Date:** _____

Directions: Read the items in both lists below and on page 142 carefully. Choose an item from List B that best matches an item from List A. Write the corresponding letter from List B on the line. You will have some left over.

List A	List B
_____ 1. minerals	**A.** Mesozoic
_____ 2. luster	**B.** Cenozoic
_____ 3. Mohs Scale	**C.** igneous rock
_____ 4. streak	**D.** volcanoes
_____ 5. sedimentary rock	**E.** powder trace
_____ 6. limestone	**F.** 6–25 miles
_____ 7. conglomerate	**G.** above the focus
_____ 8. magma	**H.** hardness
_____ 9. basalt	**I.** movement of sediment by natural causes
_____ 10. obsidian	**J.** heat
_____ 11. metamorphic rocks	**K.** made of crystals
_____ 12. young rocks	**L.** most common type of rock

GO

Rocks and Minerals

Matching Assessment *(cont.)*

List A	List B
_____ **13.** oldest rocks	**M.** rock cycle
_____ **14.** depth of Earth's crust	**N.** plates
_____ **15.** erosion	**O.** Precambrian
_____ **16.** expansion of rock	**P.** formed from shells and skeletons
_____ **17.** gravity	**Q.** light reflected by rock
_____ **18.** upper mantle	**R.** Paleozoic
_____ **19.** epicenter	**S.** individual stones
_____ **20.** rapid change	**T.** ocean floor made of this
	U. used for prehistoric tools
	V. changed rocks
	W. main force that causes landslides

Rocks and Minerals

Graphic Assessment

Name: _____   **Date:** _____

Directions: In the spaces provided, draw step-by-step illustrations that show how an igneous rock might become part of a sedimentary rock.

Step I: Show how an igneous rock is formed.

Step II: Show one way an igneous rock can change.

Step IV: Show another way an igneous rock can change.

Step III: Show one more way an igneous rock can change.

STOP

Matter

Teacher Materials

 Teacher Preparation

Before you begin this unit, photocopy and distribute the following to students:

- Data Sheets (pages 146–149)
- Student Introduction (page 150)
- Unit Vocabulary (page 151)
- Student Briefs (pages 152–157)
- Assessments (pages 158–168)

 Key Unit Concepts

- *Atoms* comprise matter.
- All objects are composed of atoms.
- How the atoms are arranged and how they behave determines the *state* of the matter.
- *Mass*, *volume*, and *density* are metric measurements of matter.
- *Mixtures* and *solutions* are combinations of substances.
- *Mixture* and *solutions* are different from each other.
- *Physical change*, *phase change*, and *chemical change* are types of changes that matter can undergo.
- *Boiling* and *melting points* are temperatures at which matter can change state.

 Discussion Topics

- What is matter?
- In what ways can states of matter be changed?

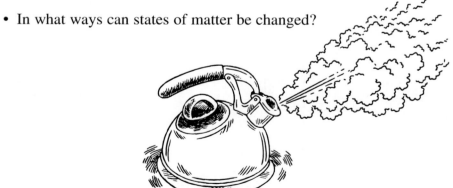

See "Generic Strategies and Activities" on pages 8 and 9 for additional strategies useful to presenting this unit.

Matter

Activities

 Brief #1: States and Measurement of Matter

- **Compare Mass:** Use a pan balance to compare the mass of different classroom objects. Record your mass comparisons on the "Mass Data Sheet" (page 146).

- **Perform an Experiment:** Select 10 objects that you think will sink in water. Fill a graduated cylinder with 50 milliliters of water. Drop each object into the cylinder and measure the height of the displaced water. Record your findings on the "Volume Data Sheet" (page 147).

- **Perform an Experiment:** Select 10 different liquids and compare their densities. Using a large glass container, pour different combinations of liquids on one another to observe density. Record your observations on the "Density Data Sheet" (page 148).

 Brief #2: Mixtures and Solutions

- **Record Mixtures and Solution:** Take a trip to the local grocery store and record 10 mixtures and solutions from each aisle of the store.

 Brief #3: How Matter Changes

- **Observe:** Put several ice cubes in a pan on the heat of the stove. Observe the phase changes that occur. Write a brief paragraph that details your observations.

- **Observe:** Remove the paper from three crayons. Place the crayons in a paper cup. In another cup, place three squares of chocolate. Leave both cups out on a warm sunny windowsill or outside. Observe them both every five minutes. Record your observations to see how long it will take for them to change into a liquid. Next, take the cups of the melted chocolate and crayons and put them into a freezer. Check every five minutes. Record your observations to see how long it will take for the crayons and the chocolate to become solid.

 Activity Center

- **Solubility:** In this activity, students will experiment to see how soluble given substances are. The following materials will be needed: salt, sugar, talcum powder, sand, soil, flour, laundry soap, a vitamin, water, and clear plastic cups. Instruct students to fill each cup halfway with water and then to drop a teaspoon of one of the substances into the water. Watch to see if the substances dissolve in the water and how long it takes for them to dissolve. Have students record their observations of the "Solubility Data Sheet" (page 149).

 Internet Resources

- *http://portal.acs.org/portal/acs/corg/content* — the website of the American Chemical Society; includes articles, activities, puzzles, and games

- *http://www.chem4kids.com/*—contains student-friendly information about chemistry

Matter

Mass Data Sheet

Name: _____ **Date:** _____

Directions: Use the chart to record mass comparisons. Write the name of an object in column one. Use the "greater than" (>), "less than" (<), or "equal to" (=) sign in column two. Write the name of the second object in column three.

Mass		
Name of Object	is > or < or =	Mass of Object
1.		
2.		
3.		
4.		
5.		
6.		
7.		
8.		
9.		
10.		

Matter

Volume Data Sheet

Name: _____   **Date:** _____

Directions: Use the chart to record an object's volume. Write the name of an object in column one. Record the object's volume in column two.

Volume	
Object	Volume
1.	
2.	
3.	
4.	
5.	
6.	
7.	
8.	
9.	
10.	

Matter

Density Data Sheet

Name: _____ **Date:** _____

Directions: Use the chart to record density comparisons. Write the name of the liquid in the first column. Use the "greater than" (>),"less than" (<), or "equal to" (=) sign in the second column to tell whether the density of the liquid was greater or less than the liquid named in column three.

Density		
Name of Liquid #1	is > or < or =	Name of Liquid #2
1.		
2.		
3.		
4.		
5.		
6.		
7.		
8.		
9.		
10.		

Matter

Solubility Data Sheet

Name: _____ **Date:** _____

Directions: Use the chart to record your observations about solubility. In the second column, tell whether each substance was soluble by writing either "yes" or "no." In the third column, write the approximate time for how long it took for the substance to dissolve.

Solubility		
Substance	Soluble?	Time
1. vitamin		
2. flour		
3. talcum powder		
4. salt		
5. sugar		
6. soil		
7. sand		
8. laundry soap		

Matter

Student Introduction: Matter Word Web

Name: _____   **Date:** _____

Directions: Use this word web to help you brainstorm characteristics of matter. What is matter? What are the different forms that matter can take? What forces change matter?

Matter

Matter

Vocabulary

1. **boiling point**—the temperature at which a substance changes into a gas

2. **chemical change**—change that turns the original matter into a different kind of matter

3. **density**—how tightly packed together the atoms in an object or substance are

4. **gas**—state of matter in which the atoms are very far apart

5. **liquid**—state of matter in which the atoms can slide past one another

6. **mass**—measurement of how much matter an object has

7. **matter**—anything that takes up space

8. **melting point**—temperature at which a substance changes into a liquid

9. **mixture**—a combination of two or more substances that can be separated

10. **phase change**—a change in the state of matter due to adding or removing energy

11. **physical change**—a change in the size, shape, or state of matter

12. **solid**—state of matter in which the atoms are packed tightly together

13. **solubility**—how easily one substance can dissolve in another

14. **solution**—combination of two or more substances that cannot be separated

15. **state**—what matter looks like and how it behaves

16. **volume**—measurement of how much space matter takes up

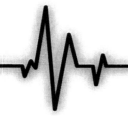

Matter

Brief #1: States and Measurement of Matter

Focus

Everything we can see is made up of microscopic particles called atoms.

Everything on Earth, whether it is living or non-living, is matter. Matter is all around you. You are matter. The chair you are sitting on is matter. Clouds, bikes, and ice cream are matter.

Often the matter all around you has a color, a taste, a smell, and a certain feel. But some matter has no color or taste or smell. Sometimes you can't even see it! But that doesn't mean it's not there. **Scientists say that matter is anything that takes up space.**

Everything we can see is made up of tiny pieces of matter called atoms. Atoms are so small that a special kind of microscope is needed to see them. How the atoms are arranged and how they move determines what matter looks like. **What matter looks like and how it behaves is called its state. There are three states of matter:**

Vocabulary
1. matter
2. state
3. solid
4. liquid
5. gas

   ✓ **solid**   ✓ **liquid**   ✓ **gas**

 Solids

One state in which matter can exist is called a solid. You can see matter in a solid state all around you. The floor of your classroom or the pages of this book are each in a solid state. **When matter is in a solid state, it means that the atoms are packed closely together.** Because there is very little room between the atoms, they do not move around very much. Matter in a solid state has a definite shape.

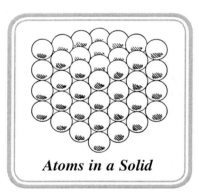

Atoms in a Solid

 Liquids

Matter can also be in a liquid state. In a liquid state, the atoms that make up the matter are not as tightly packed together. They can actually slide past one another and change places, and the bonds between them are not as strong. For this reason, matter in a liquid does not have a definite shape. Its shape changes according to the container it is in. For example, if you pour water into a glass, it takes the shape of the glass. If you pour the water from that glass into a bowl, it will take the shape of the bowl.

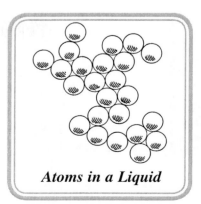

Atoms in a Liquid

Matter

Brief #1: States and Measurement of Matter *(cont.)*

 ### Gases

A third state of matter is a gas. When matter is in this state, the atoms are relatively far apart and their bonds are weak. They are not arranged in any special shape. When a gas is placed in a container, the particles in the gas will spread out as evenly as they can inside the container.

 ### How Matter Is Measured

Because matter can exist in different states, scientists have different ways of measuring it.

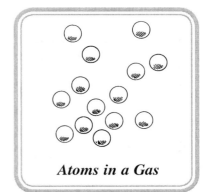

Atoms in a Gas

✓ Mass

Mass is a measurement of the amount of matter an object has. If you could count up all of the individual atoms an object contained, that would be its mass. The more mass an object has, the greater the weight the object has. The mass of an object is measured in metric units (e.g., the milligram, the gram, the kilogram). You can use a balance to measure mass.

Metric Mass

1,000 milligrams = 1 gram

1,000 grams = 1 kilogram

1,000 kilograms = 1 tonne

✓ Volume

Volume is a measurement of how much space matter takes up. Think of the tallest building you have ever seen. Scientists use volume to measure how much space that building is using. To measure the volume of a solid, you use metric units like the millimeter, the meter, and the centimeter. You can use a ruler to measure the volume of a solid.

Because liquids do not have a definite shape, to measure their volume you need to use something other than a ruler. To measure the volume of a liquid you could use a measuring cup or container. The volume of a liquid is measured in milliliters and liters.

Metric Volume of Solids

10 millimeters = 1 centimeter
100 centimeters = 1 meter
1000 meters = 1 kilometer

Metric Volume of Liquids

1,000 milliliters = 1 liter

Matter

Brief #1: States and Measurement of Matter *(cont.)*

✓ **Density**

The density of matter means how tightly packed together the atoms are in the given matter. Think of a cup of water and a cup of maple syrup. Both are liquids, but which one do you think has atoms that are more tightly packed together? If you are thinking maple syrup, you are right! In a liquid, the denser the arrangement of atoms, the thicker the liquid is.

But what about a solid? Let's say that you have two objects, and both of the objects are the exact same size. One object is made of cork; the other is made of steel.

Which object do you think has the greater density? It's the one made of steel. That's because the atoms that make up the steel are packed closer together than the atoms that make the cork. How dense an object is in relation to a liquid determines whether it sinks or floats in that liquid.

> ### Vocabulary
> 5. mass
> 6. volume
> 7. density

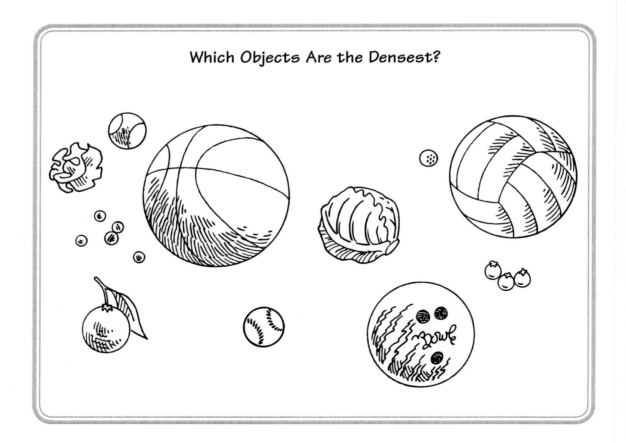

Which Objects Are the Densest?

Matter

Brief #2: Mixtures and Solutions

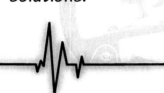

Focus

Substances can be joined together in mixtures and solutions.

You have learned that everything is made of atoms. Another word for what something is made of is *substance*. All substances—whether they are solid, liquid, or gas—can be combined or joined together with other substances. When different substances are combined, they can form a mixture or a solution.

Vocabulary

1. mixture
2. solution
3. solubility

 Mixtures

What type of cereal did you have for breakfast this morning? What substances were in it? Was it made up of corn flakes mixed with raisins? Did it have bits of different kinds of nuts? That breakfast cereal is an example of a mixture. **A mixture is a combination of two or more substances that can be separated.**

In other words, in a mixture you can see all of the substances that are a part of it. You could also take the mixture apart by separating all of the different substances that are contained in it. For example, in a big salad there may be lettuce, tomatoes, carrots, cucumbers, and peppers. You can see each substance. And if you wanted to, you could take the salad apart by removing each separate substance. The substances would still be the same as they were before they were mixed together.

 Solutions

A solution is also a combination of two or more substances—but in a solution, some of the substances that are joined together dissolve into one another. The ocean is an example of a solution. It is mainly two substances: water and salt. But when you swim in the ocean, you don't see or feel the salt. That's because the salt is dissolved in the water.

The same thing happens if you put a teaspoon of sugar into a cup of tea: the sugar dissolves in the hot tea. This doesn't mean that the sugar is no longer present. It just means that it has broken down so much that it can no longer easily be separated from the tea.

Not all substances can be dissolved in other substances. Imagine putting a spoonful of sand into a glass of water. The sand would not dissolve the way another substance might. But imagine dropping a vitamin pill into a glass of water. Eventually the pill would dissolve completely. **Solubility means how easily one substance can dissolve into another.**

Matter

Brief #3: How Matter Changes

All matter can undergo changes. There are basically three ways in which matter can change: physical change, phase change, and chemical change.

Physical Changes

Matter can undergo physical changes. **A physical change is a change in the shape, size, or state of matter.** When water changes from a solid to a gas, it has undergone a physical change. When weathering has caused a rock to be broken up into smaller pieces, it has undergone a physical change.

Focus

Matter can undergo changes.

You make physical changes to matter every day. Whenever you sharpen a pencil or use chalk to write on the blackboard, you have caused physical changes to the pencil, the chalk, and the board. When you add milk to your cereal or make the tires on your bicycle screech, you have caused all sorts of physical changes to matter.

Phase Changes

Another way in which matter can be changed is by adding or removing energy. These kinds of changes are called phase changes.

Vocabulary

1. physical change
2. phase changes
3. boiling point
4. melting point
5. chemical change

Temperature is one way to add or remove energy from matter. For example, let's say that you heat up a pan of water on the stove. The heat coming from the stove itself is adding energy to the water. The heat causes the atoms that make up the water to move around faster and faster. As the water gets hotter and hotter, the energy will increase, and the water will eventually reach its boiling point.

The boiling point of any matter is the temperature at which it turns from a liquid into a gas. Once the water reaches its boiling point, you will see steam begin to rise from the pan of water. A phase change is occurring.

Phase changes can also occur when a substance has reached its melting point. **The melting point is the temperature at which a solid becomes a liquid.** All substances—whether they are water, rocks, or lead—can undergo phase changes. Phase changes are physical changes that can be reversed. Ice can melt and become a liquid, but that liquid can also be re-frozen.

Matter

Brief #3: How Matter Changes *(cont.)*

 Chemical Changes

Matter can undergo chemical changes. **A chemical change is a change that turns the original substance into a completely different type of matter.** For example, photosynthesis is an example of a chemical change. During photosynthesis, carbon dioxide and water are changed into sugar.

Oxidation is another example of a chemical change to matter. What do you think would happen if you left your bicycle out in the rain? Eventually, a lot of the metal parts of the bike, like the chain, would begin to rust. That's because the iron or steel parts of the bike would be affected by the damp weather. This would cause a chemical reaction that would create rust. But rust is a different type of matter than steel or iron. Chemical changes cause one type of substance to turn into another type of substance.

Melting and Boiling Points (in degrees Celsius)

Substance	Melting Point	Boiling Point
gold	-1,064.58	2,856
zinc	-419.73	907
lead	-327.6	1,749
oxygen	-222.65	-182.95
nitrogen	-209.86	1195.79
water	0	100

Matter

Multiple-Choice Assessment

Name: _____   **Date:** _____

Directions: Read each question carefully. Fill in the correct answer circle.

1. What is matter?

   Ⓐ anything

   Ⓑ anything that takes up space

   Ⓒ words

   Ⓓ a form of measurement

2. What is the name for the tiny pieces of matter that make up everything we see?

   Ⓐ molecules

   Ⓑ particles

   Ⓒ air

   Ⓓ atoms

3. What makes matter solid?

   Ⓐ atoms that are far apart

   Ⓑ atoms that are heated up

   Ⓒ atoms that are close together

   Ⓓ none of these

4. When atoms can slide past each other, it means that the matter is in

   Ⓐ a liquid state.

   Ⓑ a solid state.

   Ⓒ a gaseous state.

   Ⓓ all of these

5. Why do liquids not have a definite shape?

   Ⓐ because they are packed tightly together

   Ⓑ because they have no volume

   Ⓒ because they are wet

   Ⓓ because the atoms are loosely packed together

Matter

Multiple-Choice Assessment *(cont.)*

6. What will the atoms of a gas do?

Ⓐ try to spread out evenly

Ⓑ collapse in on themselves

Ⓒ arrange themselves into tight rows of fives

Ⓓ break apart under pressure

---

7. What does mass measure?

Ⓐ the weight of an object

Ⓑ the height of an object

Ⓒ the volume of an object

Ⓓ the amount of matter an object has

---

8. What does volume measure?

Ⓐ how dense an object is

Ⓑ how much space an object takes up

Ⓒ the numbers of atoms in an object

Ⓓ none of these

---

9. What is the density of an object?

Ⓐ how much volume an object has

Ⓑ how tightly packed together the atoms in the object are

Ⓒ how quickly the object reaches boiling point

Ⓓ how quickly the matter of an reaches melting point

---

10. Which object has the lowest density?

Ⓐ rock

Ⓑ baseball

Ⓒ cork

Ⓓ book

Matter

Multiple-Choice Assessment *(cont.)*

11. What can be done to a mixture?

Ⓒ the substances can be separated out

Ⓓ the substances can be melted together

Ⓔ the substances can be dissolved together

Ⓕ the substances rust over time

---

12. Which of the following is an example of a solution?

Ⓒ a salad

Ⓓ a bowl of cereal with a banana

Ⓔ ice tea with sugar

Ⓕ all of these

---

13. What is solubility?

Ⓒ the temperature at which a solution boils

Ⓓ the temperature at which a mixture boils

Ⓔ how easily one substance dissolves into another

Ⓕ how easily one substance melts into another

---

14. If you drop a glass and it shatters, what type of change has occurred?

Ⓒ a phase change

Ⓓ a physical change

Ⓔ a chemical change

Ⓕ a rapid change

---

15. During a phase change,

Ⓒ energy may be added to matter.

Ⓓ energy may be removed from matter.

Ⓔ chemicals are added to matter.

Ⓕ both A and B

Matter

Multiple-Choice Assessment *(cont.)*

16. When matter reaches its boiling point, what phase change occurs?

   Ⓐ The matter takes the form of a solid.

   Ⓑ The matter takes the form of a liquid.

   Ⓒ The matter dissolves.

   Ⓓ The matter takes the form of a gas.

---

17. When matter reaches its melting point, what phase change occurs?

   Ⓐ The matter takes the form of a liquid.

   Ⓑ The matter takes the form of a gas.

   Ⓒ The matter takes the form of a solution.

   Ⓓ The matter takes the form of a solid.

---

18. What effect does chemical change have on matter?

   Ⓐ It turns one substance into another.

   Ⓑ It melts the matter.

   Ⓒ It dissolves the matter

   Ⓓ It destroys the matter.

---

19. Which of the following is an example of a chemical change?

   Ⓐ water turning from a liquid to a gas

   Ⓑ water turning from a solid to a liquid

   Ⓒ rust

   Ⓓ iron turning from a liquid to a gas

---

20. Why is photosynthesis an example of a chemical change?

   Ⓐ because carbon monoxide turns into sugar

   Ⓑ because carbon dioxide turns into plant food

   Ⓒ because carbon dioxide and water are converted to sugar

   Ⓓ none of these

Matter

Sentence-Completion Assessment

Name: _____   **Date:** _____

Directions: Read each statement. Fill in the word or words that best complete the sentence.

1. Anything that takes up spaces is called _____ .

2. All objects made up of _____ .

3. Matter that has atoms which are tightly packed together is in a state called a _____ .

4. The state in which atoms can slide past each other is called a _____ .

5. Liquids and gases don't have a definite _____ .

6. When a substance is a _____ , its atoms will try to spread out evenly.

7. The amount of matter an object has is called its _____ .

8. The amount of space matter takes up is called its _____ .

9. How tightly packed together the atoms in matter are is called the object's _____ .

10. An object that can float has a low _____ relative to the liquid it is in.

Matter

Sentence-Completion Assessment *(cont.)*

11. A _____ is a combination of substances that can be separated.

12. In a _____ , one or more substances dissolve into another substance.

13. _____ is how easily a substance dissolves into another substance.

14. A shattered glass is an example of a _____ change.

15. Energy is added to matter to create a _____ change.

16. When a substance reaches its boiling point, it changes into a _____ .

17. When a substance reaches its melting point, it changes into a _____ .

18. A _____ change can cause one substance to turn into another substance.

19. Rust is an example of a _____ change.

20. During _____ , carbon dioxide and water change into sugar.

Matter

True-False Assessment

Name: _____ **Date:** _____

Directions: Read each statement carefully. If the statement is true, put a **T** on the line provided. If the statement is false, put an **F** on the line provided.

_____ **1.** Matter is anything that takes up space.

_____ **2.** Objects are made up of atoms.

_____ **3.** In a solid, atoms are packed loosely together.

_____ **4.** Atoms slide past each other in a solid.

_____ **5.** Liquids have a definite shape.

_____ **6.** The atoms in gas fall in upon themselves.

_____ **7.** Mass is a measurement of how much matter an object has.

_____ **8.** Volume is a measurement of how much space an object takes up.

_____ **9.** Density is a measure of how quickly one substance dissolves into another substance.

_____ **10.** A high-density object has atoms that are packed tightly together.

_____ **11.** The substances in a mixture can't be separated.

_____ **12.** A salad is an example of a solution.

Matter

True-False Assessment *(cont.)*

_____ **13.** Solubility is how easily one substance will dissolve into another substance.

_____ **14.** Adding or removing energy from a substance is called a physical change.

_____ **15.** A change in the size and shape of a substance is called a phase change.

_____ **16.** The boiling point is the temperature at which a substance will change into a gas.

_____ **17.** All liquids have the same melting point.

_____ **18.** A chemical change causes one substance to turn into another substance.

_____ **19.** Boiling water is an example of a chemical change.

_____ **20.** Photosynthesis is an example of a chemical change.

Matter

Matching Assessment

Name: _____ **Date:** _____

Directions: Read the items in both lists below and on page 167 carefully. Choose an item from List B that best matches an item from List A. Write the corresponding letter from List B on the line. You will have some left over.

List A	List B
_____ **1.** matter	**A.** centimeters
_____ **2.** building blocks of matter	**B.** have a definite shape
_____ **3.** solids	**C.** phase change
_____ **4.** liquids	**D.** measure of space
_____ **5.** no definite shape	**E.** reversible
_____ **6.** mass	**F.** cork
_____ **7.** volume	**G.** ice tea with sugar
_____ **8.** density	**H.** loosely bonded atoms
_____ **9.** low-density object	**I.** anything that takes up space
_____ **10.** mixture	**J.** a chemical change
_____ **11.** example of a solution	**K.** substance changed to another
_____ **12.** to dissolve easily	**L.** gas

GO

Matter

Matching Assessment *(cont.)*

List A	List B
_____ **13.** change in shape and size	**M.** substance becomes gas
_____ **14.** add or remove energy	**N.** photosynthesis
_____ **15.** boiling point	**O.** atoms
_____ **16.** melting point	**P.** measure of matter
_____ **17.** chemical change	**Q.** very soluble
_____ **18.** rust	**R.** substance becomes liquid
_____ **19.** chemical change taking place inside plants	**S.** salad
_____ **20.** phase changes	**T.** how close together atoms are
	U. physical change

STOP

Matter

Graphic Assessment

Name: _____   **Date:** _____

Directions: In the space provided, draw illustrations that show how atoms look in a solid, a liquid, and a gas. Make sure to label each illustration, even the one that has been started for you.

_____

Heat

Teacher Materials

 Teacher Preparation

Before you begin this unit, photocopy and distribute the following to students:

- Student Introduction (page 171)
- Unit Vocabulary (page 172)
- Student Briefs (pages 173–175)
- Assessments (pages 176–181)

 Key Unit Concepts

- *Energy* is the ability to make, change, or do work.
- *Thermal energy* is produced from the movement of particles.
- People experience thermal energy as *heat*.
- *Temperature* is the measure of the motion of particles.
- A *thermometer* works via conduction.
- *Conduction*, *convection*, and *radiation* are ways in which thermal heat is transferred.
- A *conductor* is an object through which heat is easily transferred.
- A *convection current* is a pattern of flowing energy.

 Discussion Topics

- What type of heat is used in your house?
- Brainstorm a list of ways in which you use energy.

See "Generic Strategies and Activities" on pages 8 and 9 for additional strategies useful to presenting this unit.

Heat

Activities

 ### Brief #1: Thermal Energy

- **Make a Collage:** Using magazines and newspapers, make a collage that illustrates energy.

- **Dramatize**: Act out how particles in solids, liquids, and gases behave.

- **Role-play:** Role-play a conversation between the particles in an ice cube and the particles in a warm chocolate chip cookie. Have the particles talk specifically about what they are like and how they move.

- **Demonstrate**: Show how hot air expands and cold air contracts. Put a balloon on the neck/top of an empty two-liter bottle. (Stretch out the balloon first.) Place the bottle in a bucket of hot water. (The balloon will start to inflate.) Then place the bottle in a bucket of cold water. (The balloon will deflate.) Have students record their observations.

- **Demonstrate**: Place a thermometer in a pot of water. Then heat the water. Have students observe how the liquid in the thermometer rises as the water temperature in the water changes.

 ### Brief #2: The Movement of Heat

- **Make an Informational Poster:** Make a poster that illustrates items that are good conductors and items that are good insulators.

- **Take a Visit:** Ask your school engineer to take you on a tour of the physical plant of the school. Ask him or her to explain how the heating system of the school operates.

- **Create a Game:** Have students create a game called "Conduction, Convection, or Radiation?" Ask them to write different examples of thermal energy transfer on the backs of cards. Have students swap cards and read the examples. Students should tell whether the scenarios are examples of conduction, convection, or radiation.

   Key Words: *conductors, insulators, conduction, convection, radiation*

 ### Internet Resources

- *http://www.colorado.edu/physics/2000/bec/temperature.html* — interesting site for kids; explains temperature and absolute zero

Heat

Student Introduction: Heat Word Web

Name: _____   **Date:** _____

Directions: Use this word web to help you brainstorm characteristics of heat. What is heat? What causes heat? How is heat measured?

Heat

Heat

Vocabulary

1. **conduction**—the transfer of heat by one object touching another object

2. **conductor**—an object that allows heat to flow easily through it

3. **convection**—the movement of liquids or gasses from a warmer spot to a cooler spot

4. **convection current**—a pattern of flowing energy

5. **energy**—the ability to make things change or move or to do work

6. **heat**—thermal energy

7. **radiation**—the emission (giving off) of energy and its movement in straight lines in all directions

8. **temperature**—the measure of the motion of particles

9. **thermal energy**—the energy produced by moving particles

Heat

Brief #1: Thermal Energy

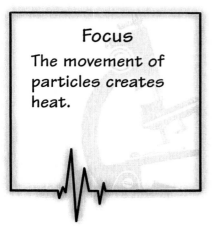

Focus

The movement of particles creates heat.

You have learned that all substances are made up of tiny particles. On Earth, substances can occur naturally in one of three states: solid, liquid, or gas. But the particles of matter are not static. They do not sit still. The particles of matter can and do move around.

Vocabulary

1. energy
2. thermal energy
3. temperature

In a solid, the particles are packed tightly together, so they can move around only a tiny bit. In a liquid, the particles can slide past each other. And in a gas, the particles can move in all different directions.

 ### Energy and Heat

Energy is the ability to make things change or move or to do work. All change or movement requires some kind of energy. For example, to get your bike to move from one place to another, you have to use energy to push on the pedals to make the bike go forward. And to make a solid change into a liquid, you have to heat it up.

All of the particles of matter are moving all of the time. But how quickly or slowly they move depends upon how much energy they have. The less energetic the particles, the less they will move. The more energetic the particles, the faster they will move. **The energy produced by the movement of particles is called thermal energy.** We feel thermal energy as heat.

You can feel this kind of energy if you rub your palms together. The energy you use to rub your palms together causes the particles on your hand to move around faster. The faster movement of the particles on your hands produces thermal energy, or heat.

 ### How a Thermometer Works

A thermometer is a tool that measures the temperature of substances. **Temperature is a measure of the motion of the particles.** If you look at a thermometer, you will see that it is made up of thin glass tubes. These glass tubes are connected at the bottom by a glass bulb. Inside of the glass bulb there is a colored liquid.

When a thermometer is placed on or in a substance that is being heated up, the liquid in the bulb of the thermometer expands in relation to the motion of the substance's particles. This will cause the liquid to expand. Because the only place for the expanded liquid to go is up through the glass tube, it will rise and show the number of degrees both in Fahrenheit and Celsius. If the particles begin to slow down, the liquid in the thermometer contracts and begins to fall back down the glass tube.

Heat

Brief #2: The Movement of Heat

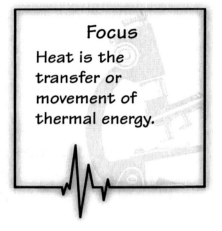

Focus

Heat is the transfer or movement of thermal energy.

Thermal energy is the heat that is produced by moving particles. But once these particles get moving, where do they go and how do they get there?

Heat is the transfer of thermal energy. In other words, the movement of energy from one place or object to another place or object is called heat. You experience this kind of transfer all of the time. On a cold day, the heat in your school building may click on and suddenly you will feel heat rising up from radiators or blowing out through vents.

Vocabulary

1. heat
2. conduction
3. conductor
4. convection
5. convection current
6. radiation

 ## Conduction

Conduction is one way in which heat is transferred from place to place. *Conduction* **means the transfer of heat by one thing touching another thing.**

For example, let's say that you were stirring a pot of soup on the stove with a metal spoon. The particles in the soup would start to heat up and move around faster. These faster-moving particles would interact with the particles on the spoon and speed them up. The heat energy would travel up the spoon, making the whole spoon warmer.

Heat energy flows more easily through certain types of materials. **A conductor is an object that allows heat to flow through it easily.** For example, heat energy will flow better through a metal spoon than through a wooden spoon. Look at all of the pots and pans in your kitchen at home. They are all made of some type of metal for this reason.

 ## Convection

Convection is the movement of liquids or gases from a warmer spot to a cooler spot. Radiators use convection to transfer heat energy. In a radiator, water is heated in a boiler. Then it is pushed through a system of pipes and into a radiator. Radiators are made of metal. The hot water heats the metal radiator, which transfers the heat to the air. The flowing heat energy from the boiler to the radiator to the air is called a convection current. **A convection current is a pattern of flowing heat energy.**

Heat

Brief #2: The Movement of Heat *(cont.)*

 ### Radiation

Another way that heat energy is transferred from one place to another is through radiation. **Radiation is the emission (giving off) of heat energy in straight lines from a heat source to the surrounding areas.** For example, the sun radiates heat in straight lines called rays. We can't touch the rays of the sun, but we can feel the heat energy from the rays. If you have ever sat in front of a space heater or a fireplace, you have felt radiation.

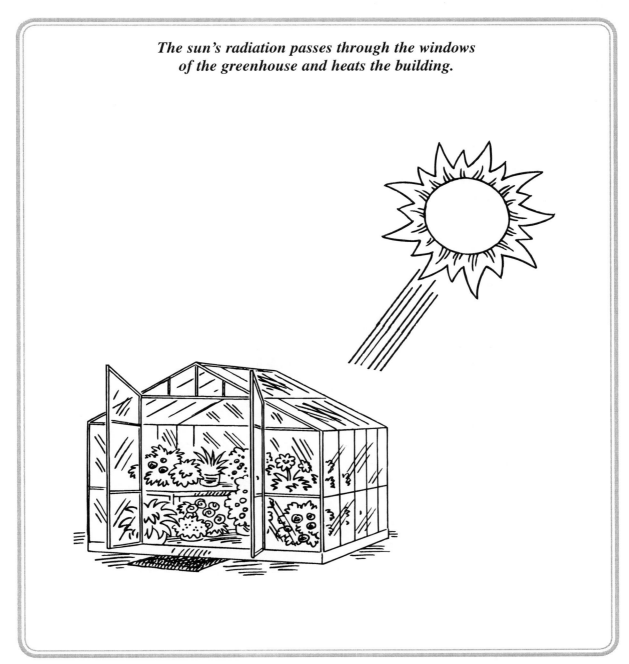

The sun's radiation passes through the windows of the greenhouse and heats the building.

Heat

Multiple-Choice Assessment

Name: _____   **Date:** _____

Directions: Read each question carefully. Fill in the correct answer circle.

1. Energy is
   - Ⓐ heat.
   - Ⓑ conduction.
   - Ⓒ radiation.
   - Ⓓ the ability to make things change.

2. What results from particles speeding up?
   - Ⓐ the sun
   - Ⓑ heat
   - Ⓒ melting point
   - Ⓓ an insulator

3. We experience thermal energy as
   - Ⓐ moving particles.
   - Ⓑ particles that do not move.
   - Ⓒ converted particles.
   - Ⓓ heat.

4. What is thermal energy?
   - Ⓐ conduction
   - Ⓑ convection
   - Ⓒ the movement of particles
   - Ⓓ none of these

5. What does a thermometer measure?
   - Ⓐ heat
   - Ⓑ temperature
   - Ⓒ thermal energy
   - Ⓓ energy

6. What does temperature measure?
   - Ⓐ how hot or cold something is
   - Ⓑ radiation
   - Ⓒ the motion of particles in a substance
   - Ⓓ all of these

Heat

Multiple-Choice Assessment *(cont.)*

7. What happens to the liquid in a thermometer?

Ⓐ it rises or falls according to the temperature

Ⓑ it conducts heat

Ⓒ if radiates heat

Ⓓ it remains the same

---

8. What is heat?

Ⓐ fire

Ⓑ thermal energy

Ⓒ the transfer of radiation

Ⓓ the transfer of a heated gas or liquid

---

9. During conduction,

Ⓐ air is moved in conduction current.

Ⓑ a liquid is moved in a conduction current.

Ⓒ heat is transferred by one thing touching another.

Ⓓ heat is insulated.

---

10. Which of the following would make a good conductor?

Ⓐ a straw mat

Ⓑ a wooden spoon

Ⓒ a glass container

Ⓓ an iron frying pan

---

11. What happens during convection?

Ⓐ One objects transfers heat to another object.

Ⓑ Liquids or gasses are moved from a warmer to a cooler spot.

Ⓒ Heat is distributed in straight lines.

Ⓓ Particles are transferred slowly.

---

12. A pattern of flowing energy is called a

Ⓐ conducted current.

Ⓑ conduction current.

Ⓒ convection current.

Ⓓ a radiated current.

---

13. Heat energy that moves in a straight line in all directions is called

Ⓐ conduction.

Ⓑ convection.

Ⓒ thermal heat.

Ⓓ radiation.

STOP

Heat

Sentence-Completion Assessment

Name: _____   **Date:** _____

Directions: Read each statement. Fill in the word or words that best complete the sentence.

1. The ability to do work is called _____ .

2. _____ is produced by the motion of particles.

3. We experience thermal energy as _____ .

4. The energy created by moving particles is called _____ energy.

5. A thermometer measures _____ .

6. The motion of particles in a substance is also called _____ .

7. The _____ in a thermometer rises or falls according to temperature.

8. Heat is the transfer of _____ energy.

9. The transfer of heat by one object touching another is called _____ .

10. An object through which heat flows easily is called a _____ .

11. When a liquid or gas moves from a warm spot to a colder spot it is called

    _____ .

12. Flowing energy is called a _____ .

13. The emission of energy that moves in straight lines in all directions is called

    _____ .

Heat

True-False Assessment

Name: _____   **Date:** _____

Directions: Read each statement carefully. If the statement is true, put a **T** on the line provided. If the statement is false, put an **F** on the line provided.

_____ **1.** Energy is the same as heat.

_____ **2.** Heat determines how quickly or slowly particles in matter move.

_____ **3.** Heat is created by moving particles.

_____ **4.** Thermal energy is radiated heat.

_____ **5.** A thermometer measures the temperature of substances.

_____ **6.** Temperature is a measure of the motion of particles.

_____ **7.** The liquid in a thermometer is meant to boil and freeze depending on the temperature of the matter it is touching.

_____ **8.** Heat is the transfer of thermal energy.

_____ **9.** For conduction to occur, objects must be touching.

_____ **10.** A conductor is an object that traps and removes thermal energy.

_____ **11.** During convection, liquids and gases are moved from a warmer to a cooler place.

_____ **12.** A pattern of flowing energy is called a radiation current.

_____ **13.** Radiation is the emission of energy that moves in straight lines in all directions.

Heat

Matching Assessment

Name: _____   **Date:** _____

Directions: Carefully read the items in both lists below. Choose an item from List B that best matches an item from List A. Write the corresponding letter from List B on the line. You will have some left over.

List A	List B
_____ **1.** energy	**A.** glass tubes
_____ **2.** causes particles to move	**B.** thermal energy
_____ **3.** cold	**C.** heat
_____ **4.** produced by particle movement	**D.** greenhouse
_____ **5.** thermometer	**E.** conduction
_____ **6.** temperature	**F.** fast-moving
_____ **7.** objects must touch	**G.** movement of liquid or gas
_____ **8.** good conductor	**H.** the ability to do work
_____ **9.** convection	**I.** temperature tool
_____ **10.** flowing energy	**J.** measure of particle motion
_____ **11.** radiation	**K.** slow-moving particles
_____ **12.** speed of hot particles	**L.** convection current
_____ **13.** part of thermometer	**M.** emission of energy in straight lines
	N. metal

Heat

Graphic Assessment

Name: _____ **Date:** _____

Directions: In the space provided, draw an illustration that shows how conduction works. Make sure to include labels.

Electricity

Teacher Materials

 Teacher Preparation

Before you begin this unit, photocopy and distribute the following to students:

- Data Sheet (page 184)
- Student Introduction (page 185)
- Unit Vocabulary (page 186)
- Student Briefs (pages 187–192)
- Assessments (pages 193–203)

 Key Unit Concepts

- Particles can have *positive*, *negative*, or *neutral* charges.
- *Charged particles* create electricity.
- "Opposites attract, likes repel" is the rule that dictates how charged particles will behave.
- An imbalance of charged particles creates *static electricity*.
- The flow of *electricity* is called a *current*.
- An *electric field* is the area around charged particles.
- A *series* and a *parallel circuit* are different ways in which electricity can move.
- *Magnetism* is a natural physical force.
- Magnetism and electricity are two parts of a single force (electromagnetism).
- The Earth is a giant magnet because of its iron core and its rotation.
- Electricity can be dangerous.

 Discussion Topics

- Discuss how you use electricity in your daily life.
- Name some ways that electricity can be dangerous or hurt you.

See "Generic Strategies and Activities" on pages 8 and 9 for additional strategies useful to presenting this unit.

Electricity

Activities

 Brief #1: Charged Matter and the Flow of Electricity

- **Role-Play:** Role-play how charged particles behave.
- **Build a Circuit:** Use batteries, wires, light bulbs, and bells to build a closed circuit.
- **Make an Informational Poster:** Create a poster that shows some materials that are good electrical conductors and others that are good electrical insulators.
- **Perform an Experiment:** Blow up several balloons. Rub the balloons on clothing, and then put them up against other balloons to demonstrate repulsion. Next, rub balloons together and put them on hair to demonstrate static electricity.

 Brief #2: Magenetism

- **Perform an Experiment:** Take a walk around your classroom, school, or house with a magnet. Make a list of things that are or are not attracted to the magnet. (Caution students to avoid using magnets on watches and computers.)
- **Perform an Experiment:** Using a magnet and iron filings, experiment to find out the shape of the magnetic field of the magnet you are using.
- **Use a Compass:** Take a neighborhood walk with a compass. As you walk, observe and take note of the various directions in which you move.

 Brief #3: Electricity and Magnetism

- **Create a Public Service Announcement (PSA):** Write and produce a PSA about electrical safety. Your announcement should be created for television or the Internet.
- **Research and List:** Research the different methods used to power generators.

 Activity Center

- **Magnetism:** Have students experiment to see how strong different magnets are. Stock the center with paper clips and with several magnets of varying strengths. Make sure the magnets are labeled with letters. Have students see how many paper clips each magnet can attract. Students can record the results of their experiment on the "Magnetism Data Sheet" (page 184).

 Internet Resources

- *http://www.bbc.co.uk/schools/scienceclips/ages/10_11/changing_circuits.shtml* — includes an animated game for kids called "Changing Circuits"
- *http://image.gsfc.nasa.gov/poetry/educator/Earth79.html* — "The Magnetic Earth" from the NASA website
- *http://www.lightningsafety.noaa.gov/* — lightning safety from the National Weather Service
- *http://www.mos.org/sln/toe/toe.html* — "Theater of Electricity" from the Boston Museum of Science; includes links to information about voltages and static electricity

Electricity

Magnetism Data Sheet

Name: _____   **Date:** _____

Directions: Use this chart to record data on the strength of the magnets provided. (See the "Activity Center" section on page 183 for more details.)

Magnet	Number of Paper Clips

Electricity

Student Introduction: Electricity Word Web

Name: _____ **Date:** _____

Directions: Use this word web to help you brainstorm characteristics of electricity. What is electricity? What causes electricity? How is electricity measured?

Electricity

Electricity

Vocabulary

1. **compass**—a tool that can help you find your way

2. **electric circuit**—looped path along which electricity flows

3. **electric current**—the movement of electricity

4. **electric field**—the area around charged particles

5. **electric force**—the attraction of oppositely-charged particles

6. **electricity**—the energy of charged particles

7. **electromagnet**—a type of magnet created by electricity and a permanent magnet

8. **magnet**—an object that can attract certain materials to it

9. **magnetic field**—the area surrounding a magnet

10. **parallel circuit**—the flow of electricity in more than one direction

11. **series circuit**—the flow of electricity in one direction only

12. **static electricity**—an imbalance of charged particles

Electricity

Brief #1: Charged Matter and the Flow of Electricity

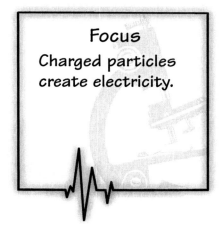

Focus
Charged particles
create electricity.

All substances are made up of atoms. And all atoms are made up of smaller things called particles. You can't see atoms or their particles with your naked eye, but they are everywhere.

Some particles in atoms are charged. Some of the particles in atoms have a positive charge. A positive charge can be shown using a plus sign (+). Some particles in atoms have a negative charge. A negative charge can be shown using a minus sign (–). And there are some particles in atoms that don't have a positive or a negative charge. These particles are called neutral. **The energy of charged particles is called electricity**. Electricity is a type of energy.

 The Behavior of Charged Particles

Charged particles can move from object to object. They do this when the positive and negative charges are not in balance. There is a rule that describes how they will move. This rule is "opposites attract, likes repel."

Suppose you have two objects. One of the objects has particles that have a positive charge. And the other object has particles that have a negative charge. These objects will attract or pull toward each other. **When two oppositely charged objects attract or pull toward each other, it is called an electric force.** A charged object can also attract a neutral object.

But what happens if two objects have the same kind of charge? Let's say that both objects have positive charges. In that case, the objects would repel, or push away, from each other.

Most of the time, the charges in objects are balanced, so no electric force is produced. For example, the book that you are holding now is not being attracted to or repelled from your hands. That's because the charged particles in both the book and your hands are balanced. But there are times when the particles in objects are not in balance. **Static electricity is produced when positive and negative changes are not in balance.**

The area around electrically charged particles is called an electric field. The electric field is the strongest close to the charged objects. The farther you get away from the charged objects, the weaker the electric field is. An electric field is invisible.

Vocabulary

1. electricity
2. electric force
3. static electricity
4. electric field
5. electric current
6. electric circuit
7. series circuit
8. parallel circuit

Fast Fact

Benjamin Franklin and Ebenezer Kinnersley were the first people to describe positive and negative charges.

Electricity

Brief #1: Charged Matter and the Flow of Electricity *(cont.)*

 ### The Movement of Electricity

The fact that electricity can move from place to place helps us to power our world. Just think about all of the things that you use in a day that use the energy of electricity!

You have learned that thermal energy can flow or move from one place to another. Electricity also moves. **The movement of electrically charged particles is an electric current.**

Electricity can move more easily though some types of material. These materials are called conductors. Materials that are good conductors are usually metals, like copper and silver. You may have noticed that many wires are made of copper.

There are other materials through which electricity does not flow that easily. These types of material—such as plastic, rubber, and wood—are known as insulators. You may also have noticed that often copper wires are covered in plastic. Copper wires are insulated or covered in plastic to stop different wires from touching each other. This would affect the electric current.

 ### Closed Circuit

Electric energy flows through your house and school along circuits. **An electric circuit is the looped path along which electricity flows.**

In the illustration below, the charged particles flow from the batteries along the copper wires, which are insulated in plastic. As the charged particles flow along the wires, they light up the bulb along the way. They continue in a loop back to the batteries. If the circuit is broken at any point, the particles will stop flowing.

This is what all of the electrical switches in your house are for. When you turn a switch on, you are opening the current and allowing the electricity to flow to a light or other electrical appliance. When you turn the switch off, you are interrupting the current. This stops the flow of electricity.

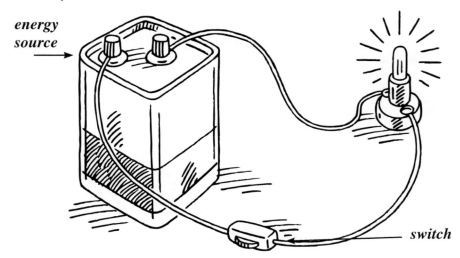

energy source →

switch

Electricity

Brief #1: Charged Matter and the Flow of Electricity *(cont.)*

 ### Series Circuit

There are different types of closed circuits. One type is called a series circuit. **In a series circuit, electricity can only flow in one direction.** If there are five lights along the loop in a series circuit and one of them blows out, it turns the circuit off and no lights along the loop will light up. You can see this happen often with long strings of holiday lights. There may be 100 bubs along a series circuit, but if one bulb burns out, none of them will light.

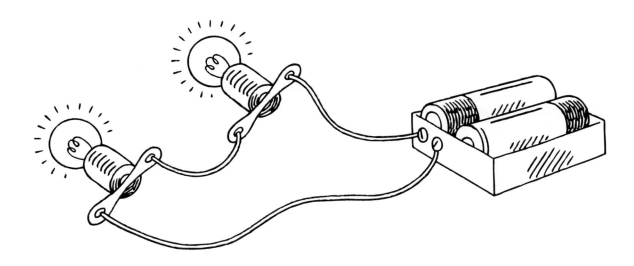

 ### Parallel Circuit

Another type of circuit is called a parallel circuit. **In a parallel circuit, there is more than one path along which the electricity can flow.** If one bulb in a parallel circuit blows out, the electricity can flow on another path so that only that one bulb doesn't light. You can see the importance of parallel circuits in your house or school. Imagine if one blown-out light bulb in your classroom meant that all the lights in the school didn't work!

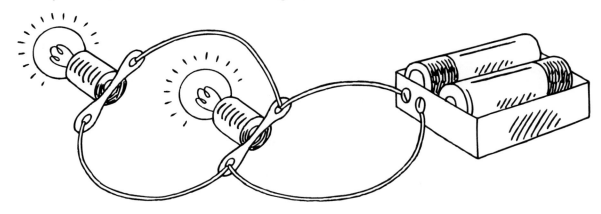

Electricity

Brief #2: Magnetism

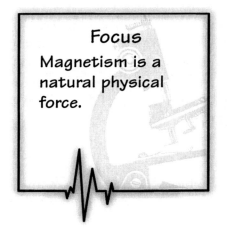

Focus

Magnetism is a natural physical force.

A magnet is an object that can attract certain materials to it. Most of these materials are different metals. Magnets especially attract iron.

All magnets have an invisible field around them. **The invisible field surrounding a magnet is called a magnetic field.**

All magnets also have a north pole and a south pole. These poles are located at the ends of the magnet. They pull in opposite directions. The north pole pulls in the direction of the north. The south pole pulls in the direction of the south. A magnet's magnetic field is strongest at its poles.

The poles of a magnet behave in predictable ways, just like electric charges. In fact, the same rule applies: opposites attract, likes repel. The north pole and the south pole of magnets will attract, but two north poles or two south poles will repel each other.

 ## The Earth as a Magnet

Planet Earth is like a gigantic magnet. The Earth is surrounded by a magnetic field. It has a north pole and a south pole. The magnetic field of the Earth is the strongest at the poles.

Scientists are not completely sure why our planet is like a magnet. Many scientists believe it is because the core of our planet is made of liquid iron. The combination of the liquid-iron core and the planet's rotation may be what is creating this magnetic field. Like all magnetic fields, the Earth's is invisible, too. But you can see it at work if you have ever used a compass.

Vocabulary

1. magnet

2. magnetic field

3. compass

A compass is a tool that can help you find your way. Like a watch, a compass has a round face, and it shows cardinal (north, south, east, west) and intermediate (northeast, southwest, etc.) directions. A compass has a needle. Because of the magnetic field of the Earth, the needle of a compass always points to north.

Electricity

Brief #3: Electricity and Magnetism

Focus

Energy created by electricity and magnetism power our world.

Electricity and magnetism are both natural forces. You may have noticed that they both share some things in common. For example, both forces are created from the movement of charged particles. Also, electricity and magnetism follow the "opposites attract, likes repel" rule. This is because they are actually two parts of a single force: electromagnetism.

Electromagnets

In the 19th century, scientists discovered that when an electric current flowed though wires, a magnetic field was created as a result. This scientific discovery lead to the invention of something called an electromagnet. **An electromagnet is a type of magnet that is created by electricity and a permanent magnet.**

One very useful thing about an electromagnet is that it allows you to control how powerful the magnetic field is by adjusting the flow of electricity. By stopping the flow of electricity through an electromagnet, you can turn the magnetic field off.

Vocabulary

1. electromagnet

Electromagnets are used in many devices that use power and have moving parts. Things like televisions, doorbells, and earphones all use electromagnets. Electromagnets are also used on a much larger scale. They can be used to lift heavy materials and also to power trains. The Maglev (which stands for *magnetic levitation)* is a train that uses the power of electromagnetism to power trains that can travel hundreds of miles per hour.

How a Doorbell Works

Pressing the button closes the electric circuit, allowing current to flow to the transformer. The transformer controls the amount of current that is sent to the electromagnet (A). Electricity flows through the coil of wire, magnetizing the electromagnet. This pulls up the contact arm (B). This arm is attached to a metal clapper that hits the bell (C). The bell makes the sound.

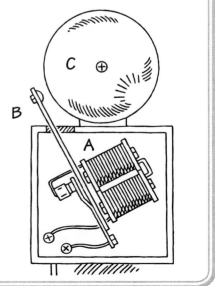

Electricity

Brief #3: Electricity and Magnetism *(cont.)*

The force of magnetism can be used to create mechanical energy (the energy to move things), which can be transformed into electrical energy. For example, by sliding or spinning wires around a magnet, you can create electricity.

Giant generators use this process to create electricity. In a generator, wires are coiled around spinning magnets. This creates large amounts of electricity.

There are lots of different ways in which generators are powered. Some generators use the power of the wind or the sun to turn the coils around giant magnets. Others use fossil fuel or nuclear power. No matter how the generators are powered, they all produce electricity by spinning metal coils around large magnets.

Electrical Safety Tips

1. Do not overload outlets with plugs.

2. Make sure there are no exposed wires on electrical cords.

3. Make sure electrical cords do not run near heaters, under rugs, or around furniture.

4. Don't carry appliances by the electrical cord.

5. Put safety caps in outlets.

6. Unplug appliances that are not in use.

7. Don't climb trees or play near power lines.

8. Do not touch power lines.

9. Don't put out an electrical fire with water.

10. If you are caught in an electrical storm, go indoors immediately.

Electricity

Multiple-Choice Assessment

Name: _____ **Date:** _____

Directions: Read each question carefully. Fill in the correct answer circle.

1. What are atoms made up of?

   Ⓐ particles

   Ⓑ nuggets

   Ⓒ cells

   Ⓓ all of these

2. What kinds of charges do particles have?

   Ⓐ negative only

   Ⓑ positive only

   Ⓒ neutral only

   Ⓓ positive, negative, and neutral

3. What is electricity?

   Ⓐ the energy of a generator

   Ⓑ the energy of charged particles

   Ⓒ another word for magnetism

   Ⓓ the energy of positively charged particles

4. What is the rule that describes how charged particles behave?

   Ⓐ opposite repel

   Ⓑ opposites attract

   Ⓒ opposites attract, likes repel

   Ⓓ opposites repel, likes attract

5. How is an electric force created?

   Ⓐ by the attraction of oppositely charged particles

   Ⓑ by the repulsion of oppositely charged particles

   Ⓒ by the power of magnetism

   Ⓓ by a generated current

Electricity

Multiple-Choice Assessment *(cont.)*

6. What would happen if two objects were both negatively charged?

　Ⓐ They would attract each other.

　Ⓑ They would create an electric current.

　Ⓒ They would repel each other.

　Ⓓ They would create a magnetic field.

---

7. How is static electricity created?

　Ⓐ by the poles of a magnet

　Ⓑ by particles that have neutral charges

　Ⓒ by mechanical energy

　Ⓓ by an imbalance of positively and negatively charged particles

---

8. What is the area around charged particles called?

　Ⓐ a magnetic field

　Ⓑ an electric field

　Ⓒ an electric force field

　Ⓓ static electricity

---

9. What is the movement of electricity called?

　Ⓐ convection current

　Ⓑ a magnetic current

　Ⓒ an electric current

　Ⓓ none of these

---

10. Why are electrical wires often made of copper?

　Ⓐ Copper is an attractive metal.

　Ⓑ Copper is a good insulator.

　Ⓒ Copper is plentiful.

　Ⓓ Copper is a good conductor.

Electricity

Multiple-Choice Assessment *(cont.)*

11. What's an insulator?

Ⓐ a material through which electricity doesn't flow easily

Ⓑ a material through which electricity flows easily

Ⓒ a light bulb

Ⓓ all of these

---

12. How does electricity flow in a series circuit?

Ⓐ in one direction

Ⓑ in a straight line

Ⓒ in an arc

Ⓓ in five directions

---

13. How does electricity flow in a parallel circuit?

Ⓐ in one direction

Ⓑ in more than one direction

Ⓒ in one parallel line

Ⓓ none of these

---

14. If one light bulb in a series circuit blows out, what happens to the other bulbs?

Ⓐ They remain lit.

Ⓑ They flicker.

Ⓒ They blink slowly.

Ⓓ They will not light up at all.

---

15. What are the ends of a magnet called?

Ⓐ poles

Ⓑ end points

Ⓒ breakers

Ⓓ fields

Electricity

Multiple-Choice Assessment *(cont.)*

16. Where is the magnetic field the strongest?

Ⓐ at the curve

Ⓑ in the middle

Ⓒ on one end

Ⓓ at the poles

---

17. What might contribute to the Earth being like a giant magnetic?

Ⓐ its copper core

Ⓑ its iron core

Ⓒ its small size

Ⓓ its large oceans

---

18. What makes an electromagnet so useful?

Ⓐ its power

Ⓑ its size

Ⓒ its current

Ⓓ the fact that you can control the size of the magnetic field

---

19. How does a generator create electricity?

Ⓐ the movement of magnets in water

Ⓑ the movement of electrical currents

Ⓒ the movement of coils around magnets

Ⓓ the movement of thermal and mechanical energy

---

20. What should you do if you are caught in an electrical storm?

Ⓐ Hide under a tree.

Ⓑ Jump in a lake.

Ⓒ Stop, drop, and roll.

Ⓓ Go indoors immediately.

Electricity

Sentence-Completion Assessment

Name: _____   **Date:** _____

Directions: Read each statement. Fill in the word or words that best complete the sentence.

1. Atoms are made up of _____ .

2. Charged particles can be _____, _____, or neutral.

3. Electricity is the energy of _____ .

4. The rule that governs how particles behave is " _____

_____ ."

5. When two oppositely charged particles attract each other, it is called an

_____ .

6. Two negatively charged particles would _____ each other.

7. _____ is created by an imbalance of positively

and negatively charged particles.

8. The area around charged particles is called a _____ .

9. An _____ is the movement of electricity.

10. Electrical wires are often made of _____ .

(GO)

Electricity

Sentence-Completion Assessment *(cont.)*

11. A material through which electricity flows easily is called a

_____ .

12. Electricity which flows in one direction is a _____ .

13. In a _____ _____

electricity flows in more than one direction.

14. Electrical wires are often insulated with _____ .

15. The ends of magnets are called _____ .

16. A _____ is the strongest at the poles.

17. The core of the Earth is made up of _____ _____ .

18. An _____ allows you to control the strength of a

magnetic field.

19. A _____ creates electricity by placing metal coils around

spinning magnets.

20. If you are caught outside in an electrical storm, you should go _____ .

STOP

Electricity

True-False Assessment

Name: _____   **Date:** _____

Directions: Read each statement carefully. If the statement is true, put a **T** on the line provided. If the statement is false, put an **F** on the line provided.

_____   **1.** Atoms are made up of particles.

_____   **2.** Particles can have positive, negative, or neutral charges.

_____   **3.** Electricity and magnetism are part of the same force.

_____   **4.** "Opposites repel, likes attract" is the rule that describes the behavior of charged particles.

_____   **5.** An electric force is created by the iron core of the Earth.

_____   **6.** Two negatively charged particles would repel each other.

_____   **7.** Static electricity is created when charged particles are imbalanced.

_____   **8.** The area around charged particles is called a magnetic field.

_____   **9.** The movement of electricity is called a particle field.

_____   **10.** Electrical wires are often made of plastic.

_____   **11.** Copper is a good conductor.

_____   **12.** In a series current, electricity flows in one direction.

Electricity

True-False Assessment *(cont.)*

_____ **13.** In a parallel circuit, electricity flows from left to right only.

_____ **14.** If a bulb in a series circuit blows out, all of the other bulbs will be affected.

_____ **15.** The ends of magnets are called poles.

_____ **16.** A magnetic field is the weakest at the poles.

_____ **17.** The iron core of the Earth may contribute to its magnetism.

_____ **18.** The strength of a magnetic field can be controlled with an electromagnet.

_____ **19.** Generators create electricity by sending electric charges to the Earth's core.

_____ **20.** If you get caught outside in an electrical storm, you should take cover under the nearest tree.

Electricity

Matching Assessment

Name: _____   **Date:** _____

Directions: Read the items in both lists below and on page 202 carefully. Choose an item from List B that best matches an item from List A. Write the corresponding letter from List B on the line. You will have some left over.

List A	List B
_____ 1. atom parts	**A.** iron core
_____ 2. particle charges	**B.** good conductor
_____ 3. electricity	**C.** compass
_____ 4. opposites attract, likes repel	**D.** particles
_____ 5. attraction of oppositely charged particles	**E.** iron
_____ 6. repulsion	**F.** electromagnet
_____ 7. imbalance of charged particles	**G.** energy of charged particles
_____ 8. electric field	**H.** movement of electricity
_____ 9. electric current	**I.** neutral charge
_____ 10. copper	**J.** pushing away
_____ 11. insulator	**K.** one-way current
	L. static electricity

GO

Electricity

Matching Assessment *(cont.)*

List A	List B
_____ **13.** parallel current	**M.** plastic
_____ **14.** poles	**N.** Ben Franklin
_____ **15.** a material attracted to magnets	**O.** electric force
_____ **16.** strongest areas of magnetic field	**P.** spinning coils around magnets
_____ **17.** contributor to Earth's magnetism	**Q.** shock
_____ **18.** tool that controls magnetic field	**R.** positive, negative, neutral
_____ **19.** generator	**S.** charged particle rule
_____ **20.** best action during an electrical storm	**T.** area around electrically charged particles
	U. more than one electrical path
	V. poles
	W. magnet ends
	X. Go inside!

Electricity

Graphic Assessment

Name: _____ **Date:** _____

Directions: In the space provided, draw an illustration of a closed circuit. Make sure to label all of the parts of the circuit.

Sound

Teacher Materials

 Teacher Preparation

Before you begin this unit, photocopy and distribute the following to students:

- Student Introduction (page 206)
- Unit Vocabulary (page 207)
- Student Briefs (pages 208–211)
- Assessments (pages 212–217)

 Key Unit Concepts

- *Sound* is created by vibrations.
- A *medium* is the matter through which a sound is traveling.
- *Compression* is where particles bunch up in a sound wave.
- *Transverse* and *longitudinal* are two types of sound waves.
- *Frequency* is the measure of how often a wave passes a specific point.
- *Wavelength* is the distance between wave crests.
- *Volume* describes how loud or soft a sound is.
- *Pitch* describes how high or low a sound is.
- *Frequency* determines how high or low a sound will be.
- The human ear is a complex organ that allows people to hear sound.
- *Decibels* are a measure of how loud a sound is (volume).

 Discussion Topics

- Brainstorm a list of pleasant and harsh sounds. What makes these particular sounds good or bad to hear?
- How can you protect your ears and hearing? Why is this important?

> See "Generic Strategies and Activities" on pages 8 and 9 for additional strategies useful to presenting this unit.

Sound

Activities

 Brief #1: The Energy of Sound

- **Demonstrate Transverse Waves:** Using a jump rope or other cord, demonstrate how transverse waves move.

- **Demonstrate Vibrations:** Bang a tuning fork against a table and then put the end of it in a bowl of water to observe the waves the vibrations produce.

- **Experiment:** Put a half cup of salt or sugar into the bottom of a plastic bowl. Cover the top of the bowl with plastic wrap. Tap gently on the plastic wrap and observe what happens to the salt or sugar. You can also experiment making sounds with different objects over the top of the bowl.

  Key Words: *transverse waves*

 Brief #2: How Sound Is Made and Heard

- **Experiment:** Experiment with several different types of musical instruments to discover what kinds of sounds they make.

- **Be a Tour Guide:** Pretend you are a tour guide and you are taking a group of visitors on a tour of the ear. Stop along the way to describe for tourists what they are seeing and the purpose of each ear part.

- **Make a List:** Make a list of places in your school that you think would produce an echo. Go to those places to see if your predictions were correct.

- **Test Your Hearing:** Invite the school nurse or an audiologist to your classroom and have them either test your hearing or explain how a hearing test works.

- **Make a Collage:** Using old magazines and newspapers, make a collage that shows animals that are known to have excellent hearing.

  Key Words: *ear, hearing, audiologist, animals with good hearing*

 Internet Resources

- *http://www.tryscience.org/experiments/experiments_japan_online.html* — a student-friendly website, includes experiments and games

Sound

Student Introduction: Sound Word Web

Name: _____ **Date:** _____

Directions: Use this word web to help you brainstorm characteristics of sound. What is sound? What causes sound?

Sound

Sound

Vocabulary

1. **compression**—the area in a sound wave where the particles are bunched up

2. **frequency**—how many waves pass a particular point in a given amount of time

3. **longitudinal wave**—a sound wave where the particles travel parallel to the sound wave

4. **medium**—the matter through which sound is traveling

5. **pitch**—how high or low a sound is

6. **sound**—the energy of vibrations

7. **transverse wave**—a sound wave in which the particles move up and down as the wave moves forward

8. **volume**—how loud or soft a sound is

9. **wavelength**—the distance between the crests of consecutive waves

Sound

Brief #1: The Energy of Sound

Focus

Sound is created by vibrations.

Our world is full of all kinds of natural forces. Many of these forces are types of energy. You have learned about heat energy and electrical energy. There is another type of energy called sound. **Sound is created by the vibrations of objects.**

You can easily test this energy by simply tapping your pencil on your desk. The tapping of one object on the other produces vibrations that make a sound that you can hear!

Vocabulary

1. sound
2. medium
3. compression
4. transverse wave
5. longitudinal wave
6. frequency
7. wavelength

 Sound Waves

Sound travels in waves. You can't see sound waves, but you can imagine what they are like. Pretend that you have thrown a stone in a small pond or lake.

The way that the water ripples away in tiny waves from where the stone landed is very much like the way that sound travels.

Sound can travel through solids, liquids, and gases. But how fast or slow the waves travel is different depending on the type of matter the sound waves are passing through. **The type of matter through which a sound is traveling is called a medium.**

Fast Fact

A sound wave that hits an object and bounces back is called an echo.

Sound is produced by the vibration of the atoms that make up the medium. The speed at which sound travels depends on particles to move the vibration along. The more tightly packed-together the particles, the quicker the sound will move. Particles are tightly packed together in solids. Because particles in water slide past one another and the particles in a gas are very far apart, sound travels more slowly in these mediums.

When sound waves pass through air, they do so in a pattern. The waves cause air particles to bunch up in certain areas. **The area where the sound waves cause the air particles to bunch up is called compression.**

Sound

Brief #1: The Energy of Sound *(cont.)*

 Sound Waves *(cont.)*

There are two basic types of sound waves.

✓ Transverse Waves

One type of sound wave is called a transverse wave. **In a transverse wave, the particles move up and down as the wave travels forward.** If you can imagine the way in which the waves in the ocean move as they approach the shore, then you can imagine a transverse sound wave.

✓ Longitudinal Waves

In a longitudinal wave, the particles travel parallel to the sound wave. If the sound wave is moving from right to left, then the particles will also move from right to left.

Sound waves can be measured. Two measures of a sound wave are frequency and wavelength.

***Frequency* means how many waves pass a particular point in a particular amount of time.** In the illustration below, you can see that three waves have passed the point that is marked with an X.

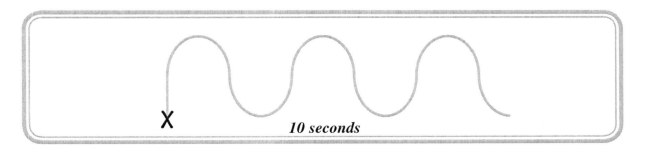

***Wavelength* means the distance between the crests of consecutive waves.** That means waves that come one after the other.

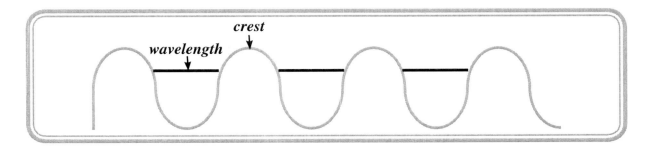

Sound

Brief #2: How Sound Is Made and Heard

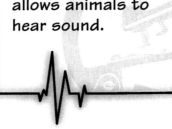

Focus

The ear is a complex organ that allows animals to hear sound.

The size and shape of an object and the material from which it is made all play a part in the volume and pitch of a sound. How near and far you are from the sound also impacts the volume.

Vocabulary

1. volume

2. pitch

 Volume

Volume is how loud or soft a sound is. Volume is the measure of the strength of a sound wave. You may have noticed that the closer you are to the source of a sound, the louder it is. And the farther you are away from it, the softer it is.

That's because when you are close to the source, the sound waves do not have to travel very far to reach you. The farther sound waves travel, the more energy they lose.

 Pitch

The pitch of a sound describes how low or high the sound will be. The faster an object vibrates, the higher it will sound. The slower an object vibrates the lower it will sound. Which instrument do you think vibrates air at the higher frequency, a violin or a tuba? If you guessed the violin, you are correct! The greater the frequency of a sound wave, the higher the pitch. Smaller objects tend to have a higher pitch than larger objects.

 The Human Ear

Our ears have three parts: the outer, middle, and inner ear. Sound enters the outer ear and travels through a kind of tunnel toward the eardrum, which is located the middle ear. The sounds waves cause the eardrum to vibrate. The vibrating eardrum then causes three tiny bones to vibrate. These bones are called the hammer, the anvil, and the stirrup because of the way they look.

The vibrations passed from the eardrum to the hammer, anvil, and stirrup continue on their journey down into the inner ear. There they cause the cochlea to vibrate. This tiny organ is filled with liquid and small hairs. The liquid inside of the cochlea vibrates and causes the tiny hairs inside of it to move. These movements are turned into signals that travel along the auditory nerve to the brain.

Look at the diagram on page 211 to see the major parts that make up the human ear.

Sound

Brief #2: How Sound Is Made and Heard *(cont.)*

 The Human Ear *(cont.)*

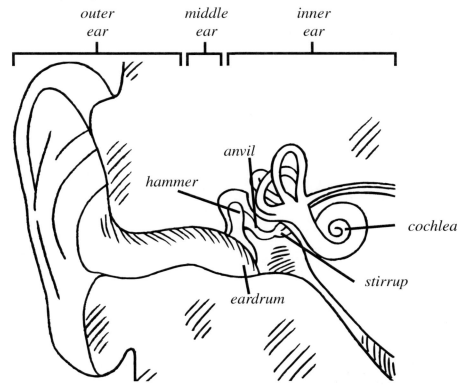

 Decibels

The volume of sound is measured in decibels. The lower the decibel level, the softer the sound. A measurement of 120 decibels or greater can be painful. People who are exposed to sound with high decibel levels over a long period of time can permanently damage their hearing.

Decibels of Everyday Sounds

Sound	Decibels
jet plane taking off	130
lawnmower	100
busy street in a big city	90
garbage disposal	80
classroom chatter	60
library	40
breathing	10

Sound

Multiple-Choice Assessment

Name: _____   **Date:** _____

Directions: Read each question carefully. Fill in the correct answer circle.

1. How is sound created?

   Ⓐ by heat

   Ⓑ by electricity

   Ⓒ by water

   Ⓓ by vibrations

2. How does sound travel?

   Ⓐ in circles

   Ⓑ through wires

   Ⓒ in a current

   Ⓓ in waves

3. What is a medium?

   Ⓐ matter through which sound travels

   Ⓑ a type of sound wave

   Ⓒ a high-pitched sound

   Ⓓ a low-pitched sound

4. The bunching up of particles in sound waves is called

   Ⓐ expansion.

   Ⓑ compression.

   Ⓒ frequency.

   Ⓓ wavelength.

5. Which is the best description of a transverse wave?

   Ⓐ a fast-moving wave

   Ⓑ a slow-moving wave

   Ⓒ a parallel wave

   Ⓓ a wave that moves up and down

Sound

Multiple-Choice Assessment *(cont.)*

6. How do particles in a longitudinal wave travel?

Ⓐ parallel to the sound wave

Ⓑ to the left of the sound wave

Ⓒ up and down

Ⓓ none of these

---

7. *Frequency* means

Ⓐ the distance between wave crests.

Ⓑ the volume of the wave.

Ⓒ how many waves pass a certain point.

Ⓓ how low or high a sound will be.

---

8. The distance between the crests of waves is called

Ⓐ wavelength.

Ⓑ compression.

Ⓒ pitch.

Ⓓ an echo.

---

9. As sound waves travel, they

Ⓐ lose energy.

Ⓑ gain energy.

Ⓒ bounce in air.

Ⓓ all of these

---

10. The pitch of a sound describes

Ⓐ how low a sound is.

Ⓑ how high a sound is.

Ⓒ the length of the wave.

Ⓓ how low or high a sound is.

---

11. If a sound is 120 decibels, it will probably be

Ⓐ high-pitched.

Ⓑ painful.

Ⓒ low-pitched.

Ⓓ all of these

Sound

Sentence-Completion Assessment

Name: _____ **Date:** _____

Directions: Read each statement. Fill in the word or words that best complete the sentence.

1. Sound is created by _____ .

2. Sound travels in _____ .

3. The matter through which sound travels is called its _____ .

4. The bunching up air particles in a sound wave is called _____ .

5. A _____ wave moves up and down as it travels.

6. Particles in a _____ wave move parallel to the sound wave.

7. How many waves pass a certain point is called _____ .

8. _____ is the distance between the crest of waves.

9. Sound waves lose _____ the farther the travel from the source of the sound.

10. The _____ is how high or low a sound is.

11. A sound of _____ or greater can be painful.

STOP

Sound

True-False Assessment

Name: _____ **Date:** _____

Directions: Read each statement carefully. If the statement is true, put a **T** on the line provided. If the statement is false, put an **F** on the line provided.

_____ **1.** Sound is created by vibrations.

_____ **2.** Sound travels in currents.

_____ **3.** The matter through which a sound travels is a circuit.

_____ **4.** Compression is the bunching up of particles in a sound wave.

_____ **5.** A transverse wave moves up and down.

_____ **6.** A longitudinal wave moves backwards.

_____ **7.** Frequency describes how big sound waves are.

_____ **8.** The distance between wave crests is called wavelength.

_____ **9.** Waves lose energy as they travel.

_____ **10.** The pitch of a sound describes how loud it is.

_____ **11.** A sound of 50 decibels would be painful to hear.

Sound

Matching Assessment

Name: _____ **Date:** _____

Directions: Read the items in both lists below carefully. Choose an item from List B that best matches an item from List A. Write the corresponding letter from List B on the line. You will have some left over.

List A	List B
_____ **1.** created by vibrations	**A.** echo
_____ **2.** how sound travels	**B.** longitudinal
_____ **3.** medium	**C.** sound
_____ **4.** bunched up particles in sound waves	**D.** painful
_____ **5.** transverse wave	**E.** eardrum
_____ **6.** parallel movement in a sound wave	**F.** up and down
_____ **7.** speed of waves past a point	**G.** how high or low
_____ **8.** wavelength	**H.** matter sound travels through
_____ **9.** result of long-distance travel of sound wave	**I.** frequency
_____ **10.** pitch	**J.** cochlea
_____ **11.** over 120 decibels	**K.** in waves
	L. compression
	M. crest to crest
	N. loss of energy

STOP

Sound

Graphic Assessment

Name: _____ **Date:** _____

Directions: In the space provided, draw an illustration of something that you think would be measured at high decibels and something that you think would be measured at low decibels. Make sure that you label what you have drawn.

Graphic-Assessment Rubric

Category	4	3	2	1
Accuracy	95% of the assigned structures are drawn accurately and are recognizable.	94–85% of the assigned structures are drawn accurately and are recognizable.	84–75% of the assigned structures are drawn accurately and are recognizable.	Less than 74% of the assigned structures are drawn accurately and are recognizable.
Labels	All items have labels, and it's clear which label goes with what.	94–85% of items have labels, and it's clear which label goes with what.	84–75% of items have labels, and it's clear which label goes with what.	Less than 74% of items have labels, and it's not clear which label goes with what.
Spelling	95% of the words are spelled correctly.	94–85% of the words are spelled correctly.	84–75% of the words are spelled correctly.	Less than 74% of the words are spelled correctly.
Knowledge Gained	95% of the items can be identified accurately.	94–85% of the items can be identified accurately.	84–75% of the items can be identified accurately.	Less than 74% of the items can be identified accurately.
Drawing Details	95% of details have been included and are clear and easy to identify.	94–85% of details have been included and are clear and easy to identify.	84–75% of details have been included and are clear and easy to identify.	Less than 74% of details have been included and are clear and easy to identify.

Answer Key

Unit #1
Multiple-Choice (pages 30–33)

1. B	11. D
2. C	12. C
3. D	13. B
4. A	14. B
5. B	15. A
6. A	16. B
7. D	17. D
8. B	18. A
9. C	19. B
10. A	20. B

Sentence-Completion (pages 34–35)

1. non-living
2. cell
3. microscope
4. nucleus
5. plant
6. six
7. Archaea, Bacteria, Fungi, Plantae
8. single
9. Fungi
10. Plants
11. Species
12. backbone
13. invertebrate
14. Mammals
15. exoskeleton
16. camouflage
17. instinct
18. hibernation
19. parents
20. life processes

True-False (pages 36–37)

1. F	11. F
2. T	12. T
3. F	13. F
4. F	14. T
5. T	15. T
6. T	16. T
7. F	17. F
8. T	18. F
9. T	19. T
10. F	20. T

Matching (pages 38–39)

1. C	11. S
2. A	12. O
3. D	13. N
4. I	14. V
5. H	15. L
6. F	16. Q
7. K	17. M
8. J	18. T
9. G	19. R
10. E	20. U

Graphic (pages 40–41)
Check the labeled diagram on page 21 for the correct answers.

Unit #2
Multiple-Choice (pages 54–57)

1. B	11. C
2. C	12. D
3. A	13. A
4. D	14. B
5. D	15. C
6. B	16. C
7. C	17. B
8. C	18. A
9. C	19. C
10. B	20. D

Sentence-Completion (pages 58–59)

1. photosynthesis
2. carbon dioxide
3. sugar
4. Oxygen
5. chlorophyll
6. sunlight
7. roots, leaves
8. Nonvascular, cell
9. tap
10. nonvascular
11. petals
12. sepals
13. pistil
14. stamens
15. anthers
16. cones
17. stamens, pistil
18. nectar
19. sperm cells, eggs
20. back, leaves

True-False (pages 60–61)

1. T	11. T
2. F	12. T
3. T	13. T
4. T	14. T
5. F	15. T
6. F	16. F
7. F	17. F
8. T	18. T
9. F	19. T
10. F	20. F

Answer Key (cont.)

Matching (pages 62–63)

1.	H	11.	E
2.	O	12.	W
3.	K	13.	V
4.	N	14.	L
5.	R	15.	G
6.	P	16.	A
7.	S	17.	J
8.	D	18.	M
9.	U	19.	T
10.	Q	20.	F

Graphic (pages 64–65)

Check graphics for accuracy and understanding.

Unit #3
Multiple-Choice (pages 82–85)

1.	D	11.	C
2.	C	12.	B
3.	B	13.	A
4.	D	14.	D
5.	B	15.	C
6.	A	16.	A
7.	C	17.	A
8.	A	18.	D
9.	D	19.	D
10.	A	20.	A

Sentence-Completion (pages 86–87)

1. system
2. living and non-living
3. 10
4. rainforest
5. population
6. community
7. niche
8. producers
9. herbivore
10. sharp
11. decomposers
12. sun
13. food web
14. natural
15. man-made
16. balance
17. landfill
18. Deforestation
19. endangered
20. extinct

True-False (pages 88–89)

1.	T	11.	T
2.	F	12.	F
3.	F	13.	T
4.	T	14.	F
5.	T	15.	T
6.	F	16.	F
7.	T	17.	F
8.	F	18.	T
9.	F	19.	F
10.	T	20.	T

Matching (pages 90–91)

1.	Q	11.	R
2.	I	12.	F
3.	E	13.	K
4.	P	14.	B
5.	S	15.	J
6.	U	16.	H
7.	L	17.	N
8.	V	18.	O
9.	M	19.	D
10.	C	20.	T

Graphic (pages 92–93)

Check graphics for accuracy and understanding. Use the food chain on page 77 as a guide.

Unit #4
Multiple-Choice (pages 107–110)

1.	D	11.	A
2.	C	12.	A
3.	B	13.	C
4.	C	14.	B
5.	A	15.	D
6.	A	16.	B
7.	D	17.	A
8.	B	18.	C
9.	B	19.	B
10.	C	20.	C

Sentence-Completion (pages 111–112)

1. five
2. Arctic
3. rocks, soil
4. hot, dry
5. glaciers
6. ice
7. liquid
8. hotter
9. evaporation, water cycle
10. precipitation
11. ground
12. air pressure
13. pressure
14. humidity
15. front
16. cirrus
17. barometer
18. depressions
19. 74
20. vortex

Answer Key (cont.)

True-False (pages 113–114)

1.	T	11.	F
2.	F	12.	T
3.	T	13.	F
4.	F	14.	F
5.	T	15.	T
6.	F	16.	T
7.	F	17.	F
8.	T	18.	F
9.	T	19.	T
10.	T	20.	F

Matching (pages 115–116)

1.	V
2.	G
3.	R
4.	U
5.	C
6.	Q
7.	J
8.	E
9.	I
10.	P
11.	M
12.	T
13.	S
14.	O
15.	B
16.	D
17.	N
18.	H
19.	L
20.	F

Graphic (page 117)

Check graphics for accuracy and understanding. Use the diagram on page 101 as a guide.

Unit #5
Multiple-Choice (pages 133–136)

1.	C	11.	C
2.	C	12.	A
3.	A	13.	B
4.	C	14.	C
5.	D	15.	A
6.	B	16.	C
7.	A	17.	B
8.	A	18.	A
9.	D	19.	D
10.	A	20.	B

Sentence-Completion (pages 137–138)

1. crystals
2. rocks
3. luster
4. hard
5. streak
6. Sedimentary
7. limestone
8. conglomerate
9. igneous
10. quickly
11. tools
12. Metamorphic
13. youngest
14. 6, 25
15. moved
16. expand
17. landslides
18. plates
19. epicenter
20. vent

True-False (pages 139–140)

1.	T	11.	F
2.	F	12.	T
3.	F	13.	F
4.	T	14.	F
5.	F	15.	T
6.	T	16.	F
7.	T	17.	T
8.	F	18.	T
9.	T	19.	F
10.	F	20.	T

Matching (pages 141–142)

1.	K	11.	V
2.	Q	12.	B
3.	H	13.	O
4.	E	14.	F
5.	L	15.	I
6.	P	16.	J
7.	S	17.	W
8.	C	18.	N
9.	T	19.	G
10.	U	20.	D

Graphic (page 143)

Check graphics for accuracy and understanding. Use the text on pages 127–128 as a guide.

Answer Key (cont.)

Unit #6
Multiple-Choice
(pages 158–161)

1. B
2. D
3. C
4. A
5. D
6. A
7. D
8. B
9. B
10. C
11. A
12. C
13. C
14. B
15. D
16. D
17. A
18. A
19. C
20. C

Sentence-Completion (pages 162–163)

1. matter
2. atoms
3. solid
4. liquid
5. shape
6. gas
7. mass
8. volume
9. density
10. density
11. mixture
12. solution
13. Solubility

14. physical
15. phase
16. gas
17. liquid
18. chemical
19. chemical
20. photosynthesis

True-False (pages 164–165)

1. T
2. T
3. F
4. F
5. F
6. F
7. T
8. T
9. F
10. T
11. F
12. F
13. T
14. F
15. F
16. T
17. F
18. T
19. F
20. T

Matching (pages 166–167)

1. I
2. O
3. B
4. H
5. L
6. P
7. D
8. T

9. F
10. S
11. G
12. Q
13. U
14. C
15. M
16. R
17. K
18. J
19. N
20. E

Graphic (page 168)

Check graphics for accuracy and understanding. Use the diagrams on pages 152–153 as a guide.

Unit #7
Multiple-Choice
(pages 176–177)

1. D
2. B
3. D
4. C
5. A
6. C
7. A
8. B
9. C
10. D
11. B
12. C
13. D

Answer Key *(cont.)*

Sentence-Completion (page 178)

1. energy
2. Heat
3. heat
4. thermal
5. temperature
6. temperature
7. liquid
8. thermal
9. conduction
10. conductor
11. convection
12. convection current
13. radiation

True-False (page 179)

1. F
2. T
3. T
4. F
5. T
6. T
7. F
8. T
9. T
10. F
11. T
12. F
13. T

Matching (page 180)

1. H
2. C
3. K
4. B
5. I
6. J
7. E
8. N
9. G
10. L
11. M
12. F
13. A

Graphic (page 181)

Check graphics for accuracy and understanding. Use the text on page 174 as a guide.

Unit #8
Multiple-Choice (pages 193–196)

1. A
2. D
3. B
4. C
5. A
6. C
7. D
8. B
9. C
10. D
11. A
12. A
13. B
14. D
15. A
16. D
17. B
18. D
19. C
20. D

Sentence-Completion (pages 197–198)

1. particles
2. positive, negative
3. charged particles
4. opposites attract, likes repel
5. electric force
6. repel
7. Static electricity
8. electric field
9. electric current
10. copper
11. conductor
12. series current
13. parallel circuit
14. plastic
15. poles
16. magnetic force
17. liquid iron
18. electromagnet
19. generator
20. inside

True-False (pages 199–200)

1. T
2. T
3. T
4. F
5. F
6. T
7. T
8. F
9. F
10. F
11. T
12. T
13. F
14. T
15. T
16. F
17. T
18. T
19. F
20. F

Answer Key *(cont.)*

Matching (pages 201–202)

1. D
2. R
3. G
4. S
5. O
6. J
7. L
8. T
9. H
10. B
11. M
12. K
13. U
14. W
15. E
16. V
17. A
18. F
19. P
20. X

Graphic (page 203)

Check graphics for accuracy and understanding. Use the diagram on page 188 as a guide.

Unit #9
Multiple-Choice (pages 212–213)

1. D
2. D
3. A
4. B
5. D
6. A
7. C
8. A
9. A
10. D
11. B

Sentence-Completion (page 214)

1. vibrations
2. waves
3. medium
4. compression
5. transverse
6. longitudinal
7. frequency
8. Wavelength
9. energy
10. pitch
11. 120

True-False (page 215)

1. T
2. F
3. F
4. T
5. T
6. F
7. F
8. T
9. T
10. F
11. F

Matching (page 216)

1. C
2. K
3. H
4. L
5. F
6. B
7. I
8. M
9. N
10. G
11. D

Graphic (page 217)

Check graphics for understanding of the concept.